# POPLORE

FOLK AND POP IN AMERICAN CULTURE

# POPLORE

## GENE BLUESTEIN

University of Massachusetts Press · Amherst

This book is published with the support and cooperation
of the University of Massachusetts at Boston.

Designed by Rebecca S. Neimark
Set in ITC Cheltenham and Emigre Matrix by Keystone Typesetting, Inc.
Printed and bound by Thomson-Shore, Inc.

Library of Congress Cataloging-in-Publication Data
Bluestein, Gene, 1928–
Poplore : folk and pop in American culture / Gene Bluestein.
p.   cm.
Includes bibliographical references (p.     ) and index.
ISBN 0–87023–903–1 (cloth : alk. paper). — ISBN 0–87023–904–X (pbk. : alk. paper)
1. Folklore—United States—History and criticism.
2. Popular culture—United States.   3. United States—Social life and customs.
4. Herder, Johann Gottfried, 1744–1803—Contributions in folklore.   I. Title.
GR105.B483      1994
398′.0973—dc20      93–43614
CIP
British Library Cataloguing in Publication data are available.

For the Poplorists
and to the memory of
Blackie Davidman
1928–1989

*If anyone should ask you*
*Who composed this song,*
*Tell 'em it was Huddie Ledbetter.*
*He's been here and gone.*
—Huddie Ledbetter

# Contents

# CONTENTS

# Preface

There is still a good deal of controversy about issues of diversity and multiculturalism in the United States, but I argue here that the question should be moot. We are and always have been a mosaic of diverse cultures and traditions. The task is to show how these elements were melded into the variegated yet unified society we have become and how that history should be understood today. It is ironic, as I shall show here, that much of the unity in our culture derives from a widespread appreciation of black culture, especially the music and dance created by African Americans. Although our best critics have always maintained that demands for homogeneity and conformity are the real threats to a vigorous and responsive society in the United States, arguments for versions of the "melting pot" still persist. Even so sophisticated a historian as John Higham is perplexed by the issue, arguing that "America is more than a federation of minorities. It encompasses many millions who will never conceive of themselves in those terms. Americans are a people, molded by processes of assimilation. An adequate theory of American culture will have to address the reality of assimilation as well as the persistence of differences ("Multiculturalism and Universalism: A History and Critique," *American Quarterly* 45 [1993]: 195–219). I find the solution to this apparent dilemma in syncretism, the process in which strong forces result in a new product that embodies elements from all the components. That is precisely how the quality of American cultural life has been forged.

One would think that professional folklorists, as cultural researchers, would know this better than anyone. But something like an old boys' network in the field seems to have kept practitioners insulated from materials and approaches that contradict narrow, superannuated views. I suspect that this study will engender hostility from some mainline folklorists, many of whom are students or followers of Richard M. Dorson. (My longstanding disagreements with Dorson's "conservative" views, and his with mine, are described in the pages that follow.) One anonymous reader of the manuscript for another publisher was, I infer, of this conventional persuasion. He "sincerely" believed that his sentiments reflected the "likely reactions of folklorists at the forefront of the discipline," but, by his own admission, could offer no "constructive criticism" and maintained that no amount of revision would render the study publishable. Redemption, it appears, is impossible unless one is among the elect.

In fact, several sections of the book have been vetted and previously published. A version of chapter one appeared in the *Journal of American Culture* and won the Carl Bode Award of the American Culture Association in 1990 "in recognition of excellence of scholarship." It was deemed "a fresh and significant reevaluation of the definition of folk and folklore in the American experience."

A good part of the discussion of Herder in chapter 2 was published as "Johann Gottfried von Herder" in *European Writers,* vol. 4: *The Age of Reason and the Enlightenment,* George Stade, editor-in-chief, pp. 639–60. Copyright 1984 Charles Scribner's Sons. Used by permission of Charles Scribner's Sons, an imprint of Macmillan Publishing Company.

The interview with Moe Asch first appeared in *American Music,* a journal published by the Sonneck Society and the University of Illinois Press.

The material on Buell Kazee appeared in a slightly edited form in *The Old-Time Herald: A Magazine Dedicated to Old-Time Music,"* edited by Alice Gerrard and published in Durham, North Carolina.

They are used here by permission.

Although I talk a good deal about folklore, I am interested in the field mainly as an index of values in American culture. Indeed it is important to note the difference between the approaches of conventional folklorists and those, like me, who are devoted to American studies. Although many of the former still tend to operate in a closed field and even recommend a kind of licensing of practitioners, the latter insist on keeping options open and vistas unlimited. Such a view of American studies offers valuable checks and balances that help prevent one's ideological commitments from overwhelming one's common sense.

I have been lucky to have the advice of the Bluestein family, those sweet singers and honest critics who have tried to keep this study interesting and readable. Jemmy Bluestein spent many hours working over the manuscript with those aims in mind. William T. Lhamon, Jr., raised some important issues in a valuable critique. Kermit Vanderbilt provided a judicious and perceptive reading at a crucial moment in the life of the manuscript. Several anonymous readers provided helpful comments. From the beginning of my career, I have relied on insights provided by Charles Seeger, who has always been light years ahead of everyone.

Paul Wright of the University of Massachusetts Press kept his commitment to this study through stages of negotiation that would have defeated individuals with less courage and integrity.

It is a pleasure to express my thanks to Kathryn Grover, who edited the manuscript for the press and made many helpful suggestions.

My wife, Ellie, has always been my first and best reader. Without her support and intelligence none of my projects would have come to fruition.

I am happy to acknowledge with thanks the responses to my work by colleagues in a variety of fields. The shortcomings of this study, of course, are exclusively my own responsibility.

Fresno, California

# POPLORE

# Introduction

"Each age," Emerson argued in *The American Scholar,* "must write its own books; or rather, each generation for the next succeeding. The books of an older period will not fit this." There comes a time in each generation when all areas of interest are subject to the truth of Emerson's insight. We are in the midst of just such a revisionary moment and its impact can be seen in literature, in the arts, and in social studies. Folklore is just beginning to feel the invigorating energy of re-vision, looking closely and critically at its fundamental positions and ideological commitments. One reason for the re-evaluation coming late, as I will try to show, is the enduring influence in the discipline of a belief that the folk (as well as their lore) are conservative, in process as well as in politics. The folk process, that is, implies slow change over long periods of time, as well as resistance to alteration of texts and music. Starting with this deeply ingrained view, students of folk arts have tended to look past the reality of American experience, repeating the assumptions and following the examples of the founders of a folk theory inferred from quite different backgrounds than our own. That is why I begin this study with an attempt to define the meaning of folklore—a task that folklorists have generally abandoned, insisting, on the one hand, that it is an impossible assignment while, on the other, accepting the conceptions developed a hundred years ago by British and European scholars looking at the matrix of their own cultures.

At the same time, I have continued to develop my interest in the eighteenth-century inventor of folk ideology, Johann Gottfried

Herder. Herder in my view remains a widely misunderstood figure and misconstrued influence, largely because folklorists here and abroad have attributed to his humane, international values all the dread connotations of "romantic nationalism," a euphemism in folk circles for chauvinism and provincial prejudice. Even if it were not for the interest in Herder's authentic positions by American thinkers from Emerson to Constance Rourke, his insights into the relationships between folklore and nationalism, folk and formal artistic expression, relativism and universalism warrant special attention and have considerable utility in any attempt to characterize the nature of American culture and its folk sources.

This is also a study in syncretism, a development in which strong elements in two or more cultures combine to create a new and different product in which none is overwhelmed. It is also an examination of one of the great paradoxes in American culture. Despite recent efforts to overcome discrimination, the United States remains one of the most socially segregated countries in the world, especially for blacks and whites. In every area of our lives African Americans and whites live on separate and unequal scales—in education, employment, housing, and all the other main indices of well-being, including life expectancy.[1] But in connection with music and dance, the United States is clearly the most integrated society in the world. White people apparently cannot live without black music (although, as their reactions to rap music and earlier to jazz suggest, they often make a fuss about the earthiness of the materials), and they cannot resist adopting every black dance as it is created in the African-American communities of our land. (The playfulness of black speech sometimes goes unnoticed, as in the case of widespread admiration in the white middle-class community for "the black bottom.")[2]

There is no doubt that certain black elements are central to our musical heritage, notably "hot rhythm," a term difficult to define but quite clear in its manifestation. The blues—a distinctly African-American form—is the foundation of almost all popular, commercial and jazz developments.[3] One could say that jazz from its beginnings also shows the merging of a white, Tin Pan Alley commercial tradition with an African-American improvisatory folk-based[4] style.

Moreover, in developing cultural dynamics, nothing African sounds exactly like its American progeny until American material returns to the motherlands to generate and regenerate High Life, Calypso, Reggae, and the many varieties of World Beat music.

Despite generations of enforced segregation, the history of our music and dance shows this consistent interaction, not only between black and white traditions, but also with Latino and a number of other "ethnic" cultures as well. Although our music and dance show this connection from almost the beginning of our history, critics are only now acknowledging other comparable developments, including the impact of folk sources on literary expression.[5] As Henry Louis Gates, Jr., has argued, there can be no return to the time "when men were men, and men were white, when scholar-critics were white men, and when women and persons of color were voiceless, faceless servants and laborers, pouring tea and filling brandy snifters in the board rooms of old boys' clubs."[6]

Given the disrupted background of African-American culture, scholars have often noted that the survival of the African heritage is nothing short of a miracle. The characteristic fate of a minority tradition when it encounters a dominant culture is usually its assimilation; a powerful major force surely can be expected to overwhelm a weaker one. An important instance is the fate Native American traditions suffered in the hands of early collectors and interpreters.

In 1855 Henry Wadsworth Longfellow published what he considered to be an American epic, using Native American culture as the equivalent of a "barbaric" underpinning for the national character. Longfellow's acquaintance with Henry Rowe Schoolcraft's early research into the history and literature of Indian tribal cultures (beginning in 1839) provided him with just the material he was looking for to construct the narrative. Longfellow had also read a German metrical translation of the Finnish epic, the *Kalevala,* a work composed by Elias Lönnrott that used Finnish folk themes. Its singsong meter works effectively in Finnish, but its four-beat trochaic line—"By the shores of Gitche Gumee, / By the shining Big-Sea-Water"—quickly becomes ludicrous in English. Longfellow thought the Finns, like Native Americans, were an appropriately "barbaric" group who would contribute the savage requirements essential to epic expression. But Arnold Krupat has pointed out the flaw in his approach:

> Longfellow's Hiawatha comfortably counsels the people to abandon the old ways and adapt themselves to the coming of "civilization," and he does so in a meter that only "civilization" can provide. It is necessary, of course, to mention Longfellow in any consideration of possible Indian influence on American literature, but *The Song of Hiawatha,* in fact, shows no such influence at all. Longfellow did not make use of Schoolcraft's Chippewa translations (themselves mostly "civilized" in their formal conventions), nor did he have any sense of his own about what Native American literary composition might actually be like or whether it might somehow stand without Finnish support and supplementation. The admission of *Hiawatha* into the American canon had nothing to do with the possibility of expanding the canon; *Hiawatha* merely assimilates the Indian to the persisting Eurocentrism of the east."[7]

Whereas Longfellow's poem was an instant best-seller, Whitman's *Leaves of Grass,* published the same year, was notoriously unsuccessful. Its "Song of Myself," Whitman explained, was not an epic but a "psalm of the republic"; not surprisingly, it was very conscious of the American Indian presence. Later in his life Whitman wrote: "As to our aboriginal or Indian population . . . I know it seems to be agreed that they must gradually dwindle as time rolls on, and in a few generations more leave only a reminiscence, a blank. But I am not at all clear about that. As America, from its many far-back sources and current supplies, develops, adapts, entwines, faithfully identifies its own—are we to see it cheerfully accepting and using all the contributions of foreign lands from the whole outside globe—and then rejecting the only ones distinctively its own—the autochthonic ones?"[8]

By contrast to the fate of native culture in the United States, black culture from Africa has not only survived but has in fact become the main source of many striking elements in American culture. W. E. B. Du Bois noted early in this century that story and song are among the main gifts to America from its black people:

> Before the Pilgrims landed we were here. Here we have brought our three gifts and mingled them with yours: a gift of story and song— soft, stirring melody in an ill-harmonized and unmelodious land; the

gift of sweat and brawn to beat back the wilderness, conquer the soil, and lay the foundations of this vast economic empire two hundred years earlier than your weak hands could have done it; the third, a gift of the Spirit. . . . Our song, our toil, our cheer, and warning have been given to this nation in blood-brotherhood. Are not these gifts worth the giving? Is not this work and striving? Would America have been America without her Negro people?[9]

The mingling that Du Bois identified has not been limited to the contributions of African Americans. The United States has been granted cultural rewards from many groups that have migrated here from all parts of the world, the people dreaming of America and often unconsciously marking the outlines of the dream in their own unique expression. I can think of no other example where the minorities in a large country have put their stamp so clearly on the character and quality of the national culture; minorities throughout the rest of the world usually remain self-contained and separate in regional enclaves, valued primarily for their exotic features, or are absorbed in a "melting pot."

The United States has experienced a momentous process of syncretism. In linguistics, syncretism refers to "the fusion into one of two or more originally different inflectional forms." In general it means "a reconciliation of diverse beliefs, practices or systems of various tenets or principles."[10] What has taken place in the United States as a result of widespread syncretism is quite different from what generations of folklorists have taught us to recognize as the folk process—anonymity, slow change over long periods of time, and isolation from popular, formal, and commercial influences. Held to these criteria, the nature of expression in the United States simply does not qualify as authentic folk tradition. Our unique combinations—including mixtures of Anglo-Celtic, African-American, Latino, Afro-Cuban, and many others—are distinguished mainly by the direct and controlling influences of popular and commercial sources whose products often show the stamp of clearly defined individual personalities. Folklorists have never been able to deny these influences, but they habitually either underplay their effects or declare the subjects out of bounds. So even to this day, major artists of the past (as well as such contemporaries as Woody Guthrie and Pete Seeger) are either excluded from evaluation or se-

5

lectively examined in such a way as to avoid evidence of such issues as the influence of non-folk sources on their work and the powerful individualism of their expression.

Folklore, in my view, needs to be understood in a new way. Here I use the term *poplore* as a positive rather than a pejorative expression. Folklorists generally consider poplore an invasion of folk tradition by insidious popular and commercial materials. Archie Green has explained that poplore comprises materials "which are disseminated by commercial entertainment and related media, but which function traditionally" and has tried to distinguish such materials from folklore. "Such provocative forms as graffiti, ski songs, and 'skinflicks' are intrinsically interesting, but their creators are not necessarily folk or even folk-like," Green has argued. "Does undergraduate sorority singing really bind its members together in the same fashion as toil in the bowels of the earth binds coal miners? Miners, neither tribal nor rural, are sufficiently linked by the centripetal nature of their work to behave, in part, as the peasantry does."[11] In his discussion of collector George Korson's work among coal miners, Green has maintained that the "theme of purity against contamination—constantly prevalent in folkloric thinking—persisted with Korson for decades." According to Green, Korson rejected the work of "such bards as Aunt Molly Jackson" despite their folk origins because they were also consciously political. "When I found that [a ballad] had been written by an outsider I didn't use it," Korson acknowledged. "I had to be especially careful because in the 1920's and 1930's the Communists were making a determined effort to capture the United Mine Workers of America, and some of the songs were composed by their organizers. When I was sure of this source—and I had ways of finding out—I just didn't use the song in my collection" (18).

More recently, sociologists such as John Fiske have noted that "in an industrial society the only resources from which the subordinates can make their own subcultures are those provided by the system that subordinates them. There is no 'authentic' folk culture to provide an alternative, and so popular culture is necessarily the art of making do with what is available."[12] Such comments are characteristic of the British school of Cultural Studies, which has been a strong influence on popular culture critics, many of whom provide important insights into the complex relations of pop, commercial, and "capitalist consumerism." Their work is often useful for explaining the intricacy of popular arts, which all too often are looked at in oversimplified and condescending ways. Andrew Ross, for example, has argued strongly against the idea that "the products of commercial music are somehow less truthful as a result of their appeal to as broad an audience as possible." Such arguments, he has noted, reinforce "the ideology of the superiority of 'noncommercial' folk spontaneity, which ignores the fact that commercial and contractual relations enter into *all* realms of musical entertainment, or at least wherever music is performed in order to make a living."[13] Ross is also very much aware of the political issues that persist within the framework of popular culture expression, even if they are sometimes not the result of conscious ideological programs.

But Ross has also argued that the earlier folk-like elements in American tradition have been inconsequential in the ensuing development of popular culture and what I call poplore. Ross has cited his own background as

> an erstwhile Scot, whose first national-popular culture is an immensely fabricated skein of folk myths and *havers,* stitched up by monarchical and crypto-nationalist ceremony into the most fantastic mummery of tartan shapes and guises—a folk-royal culture that is a colorful but irritating and mostly alien presence, with which an increasingly deindustrialized people has learned to peacefully coexist, not however without some degree of cynical endurance and verbally armed resistance. . . . Eight years of living now in a republic with no such official folkloric tradition to speak of has meant coming to terms with the quite different ways in which the overlap between culture and authority establishes its sense of popular sovereignty within everyday life, and reshapes, molecule by molecule, one's identity and subjectivity.[14]

As I try to show here, the folkloristic elements in American culture are crucial factors in determining the nature of our popular tradition and, moreover, are constantly being rediscovered in their pre-pop forms.

George Lipsitz, another culture studies critic, has pointed out that popular culture is easier to define by what it is not—not "the

Enlightenment culture of 'beauty and truth'" nor "the isolated 'folk' cultures studied by anthropologists and folklorists."[15] Commercial culture since the end of World War II has developed from what Lipsitz has termed "identifiable conditions of possibility. These conditions are not an 'aesthetic,' or a finite set of rules guiding artistic production and reception; they are not inherently 'progressive' practices guaranteed to advance struggles against exploitation and hierarchy, wherever they appear; they are not pure, authentic, or transcendent by themselves. They are historically specific elements within a commercial culture that allow for the expression of collective popular memory and the reworking of tradition."[16]

Other culture studies critics have hinted at the necessity to comprehend popular materials in some definition of folk expression. Reebee Garafalo has observed that the sociological and everyday meanings of the terms *folk, popular,* and *mass* differ greatly: "Woody Guthrie, for example, is remembered as a folk artist. But *folk* in this sense is a marketing category that was created by the music industry, in part, to separate performers like Guthrie from those producing commercial country music. In the sociological use of the term, Guthrie exhibited none of the characteristics of a folk performer. He was a known artist. He was a paid professional. He was not a member of the community he sang about. He appeared in formal settings that separated artist from audience. It would be more correct to say that Guthrie was a popular artist performing in a folkloric idiom."[17]

In contrast to the understandings popular culture critics have advanced, I want to redefine the term poplore to mean the tradition developed early in our history in which creative individuals integrated sources similar to those appearing in older, more traditional cultures with popular or commercial elements. Their artistry expresses itself within the framework of a folk process that, instead of developing over long periods, changes very quickly. Whether consciously or incidentally, they revive strong stylistic elements and values from the matrix of our "traditional" culture.[18] The popularization of the folk banjo by minstrels in the nineteenth century and a similar revival in our own time by Pete Seeger and Earl Scruggs are compelling examples. Their influence on a wide audience was made possible by recordings, especially those propagated by Moe Asch and his Folkways company, which specialized in the work of "traditional" and "ethnic" performers.

Unlike patterns of folk expression in older societies, for us the balance between the individual and the community is often tipped clearly toward the former; poplorists,[19] however, deliberately emphasize the collective values of the society that do not vanish into the anonymity folklorists have led us to expect when the folk process operates. Such commitments as folklorists have made to the association of folklore with anonymity, or, indeed, as poplorists have made to individual expression, can rarely be maintained without strong ideological implications. The theory of poplore derives ultimately from American ideas of radical egalitarianism, which are always just below the surface of our political institutions.[20] And unlike many mainline folklorists, poplorists are consciously progressive and even sometimes openly radical; like Pete Seeger and Woody Guthrie, they often embrace socialist ideologies.

As Herder was among the first to argue, folk arts are the essential sources of a nation's culture. Since those controlling ideas emanate from the common people (the peasantry in Herder's time), they lead very directly to a democratic ideology that includes arguments against discrimination—political, economic, or racial. This is the position I appropriate and explicate at length in Chapters 2 and 3. Those commitments to the voices of the folk as they express themselves in what I call poplore have transported elements from American culture to a position of prominence in freedom movements everywhere in the world. Poplore consolidates the traditional values of our democratic heritage with the individualism always implicit in American thought. This merger is clearly contradictory to conventional estimates of folk expression, which assume that the personal will disappear in the necessities of communalism. In poplore, the balance shifts toward the individual. Given the nature of the American experience, that folklorists should continually attempt to convince us otherwise is curious. My discussion of the work and continuing influence of the conservative folklorist Richard M. Dorson tries to show how most poplorists consciously expand the democratic ideology of our nation in positions that range from minimal social amelioration to outright socialist commitments, despite the continuing arguments from Dorson and his many students that eschew any association between folk and political expression.

Despite their emphasis on authorship, poplorists nevertheless speak with more than their own voices. As Arnold Krupat has explained, "In Native American autobiography the self most typically is not constituted by the achievement of a distinctive, special voice that separates it from others, but rather, by the achievement of a particular placement in relation to the many voices without which it could not exist" (133). This dialogic engagement (which Krupat relates to the views of Mikhail Bakhtin) occurs not only in folk tradition but in contemporary Native American literature as well, where the author is "collectively rather than individually constituted."[21] Such also is precisely the method of poplore.

I argue that music reveals most clearly the way folk expression has been uniquely developed in our country. As Charles Seeger has explained, the last hundred years has shown "that the process of oral transmission has far greater vitality than the repertory it has built. Though it may not have incorporated new materials as fast as the old were lost, we cannot claim that it has failed to preserve its integrity and continued, against unusual odds, its age-old digestive, formative function even though manifestly crippled by the changed social conditions." Seeger has further argued that despite the basic reorganization of modern society, "The vast majorities of the populations of even the most highly industrialized societies are still musically illiterate. Music can be *made for* these majorities through written techniques. But it can still be *made by* them only through oral techniques. . . . The resurgence of orally learned singing and instrument playing here has even been implemented with industrial products that originally were considered to be militating against this practice."[22] As I will show later, such "industrial products" as phonograph recordings have been a major poplore resource.

If music has been irresistible to the nation, literary influences have been slower to make themselves felt. But it is clear that our literary expression has also been part of a movement that consciously uses folklore as a source of esthetic and political values. Contemporary critics are beginning to look at the limitations of the

American canon, which often ignores folk elements. Moreover, the strong innovations of American culture are now connected to a network of world music and international poplore that syncretizes its traditional sources with mesmerizing rhythms from all levels of culture. I suggest that we have arrived at the beginning of that international stage of human expression that Herder foresaw as the inevitable result of nationalism. What will concern me most in this study is the way in which folk and popular culture have combined to define the nature of that new world in the making. In the process, I hope to revise the accepted notions of the nature of folk expression in our country and show in some detail what we have inherited and what we have created on our own terms.

# ONE

## What Is Folk?

The study of folklore began among an influential group of genteel British and American amateur collectors who flourished around the turn of the century. Since that time folklore has always implied a long period of gradual development that results in narrative variation and ultimately in anonymity. This premise underlies the idea that the folk collectively determines what will survive and what will fall away. This notion embraces the notably Darwinian implication that in folklore, the survivors are the fittest, and this conception of the field has often led it to a close parallel with Social Darwinism.[1] Implicitly, folklorists have believed that folk materials were meant to persist. The less capable (meaning, usually, the popular materials) are thus defined as ephemeral, destined to fade away like undesirable genetic characteristics.[2]

This view of folklore is almost totally irrelevant for the American experience. Too many folklorists have simply accepted these original premises without questioning whether they make sense for our culture, which is a very different one from that in which the founders of British folklore theory worked. An examination of some reigning conceptions of folklore, its origins, and its significance in contemporary society will make plain why a reformation of the early folk ideology[3] is long overdue, and why the United States needs a different model for the idea of folk and folklore.

It is strange that at this late date definitions of folk are still difficult to come by. Folklorists are like physicists faced with the problem of defining matter. They know matter is there; they can see its tracks and measure its impact, especially when it is blown up. But no one can say exactly what or even where it is, except in a general way. Faced with a similar demand, folklorists often refer to the twenty-one separate definitions published in the *Funk and Wagnalls Standard Dictionary of Folklore, Mythology, and Legend,* easily found in most libraries.[4] But if a specialized encyclopedia includes so many different approaches, what hope is there for a precise definition? Jan Harold Brunvand has noted that regardless of the definitions they use, most folklorists agree that five essential qualities characterize "true folklore": it must be oral, traditional, anonymous, "formularized," and present in different versions. In summary, Brunvand has defined folklore as "those materials in culture that circulate traditionally among members of any group in different versions, whether in oral form or by means of customary example."[5] But because he does not define such key words as "traditional," this definition is far from fully satisfactory. Like many American folklorists, Brunvand has concentrated on "Anglo-American sources," an approach that shows clearly the influence of the founding British school and puts aside the significance of black and other "ethnic" materials.

Another characteristic approach among folklorists is to suggest that a country like ours, with so little history and no significant "primitive" groups, obviously cannot be the locale of serious folk development.[6] One collection of folklore from the 1970s has asserted that "folk" in this country means "pretty much what one wants it to mean, though most Americans today, because of their exposure to education and the mass media, are too sophisticated to be so identified." This analysis puts forth the idea that there is folklore in America but no American folklore; because the United States is a relatively young country and because it takes a significant period of time for folklore to develop, one cannot expect to find a national folk tradition here.

> Despite the fact that during its brief history this country has not produced a national folk culture and contains very few people who may, by strict definition, be called "folk," America possesses a rich and varied folklore. . . . Strictly speaking the folk are those people who express themselves artistically without recourse to reading and writing, who are either primitives or separated from the educated

portion of society by bonds which color their every moment. Such a conservative definition has certain implications. First, it suggests that if books, newspapers, television, radio, and the like are a normal part of a people's daily existence, these people are not folk. Second, it suggests that folk art, passed along by word of mouth and retained by memory, is in a state of flux, is ever being changed and re-created. Third, it suggests that in a country as large, diffuse, and limited in the time span of its history as the United States, a national folk culture will not evolve; rather there will be a number of fragmented, parochial folk groups taking their identity from a combination of regional, ethnic, and occupational characteristics.[7]

Because individuals from cultures with a long folk history have immigrated to the United States and brought their folk materials with them, folklore exists in this country. But these folk traditions, it is asserted, function "parochially" and do not become national in any sense. This approach usually compares—invidiously—the folk materials of the United States with those of the Old World. The latter are pure folk while ours are tainted, usually through the influences of education and mass or popular material.[8] The term "conservative" is important not only as a description of the folk process but also in its political sense, its association of folk with the status quo and opposition to social and political radicalism of any kind. Such definitions contain an obvious paradox: while folklorists have often described folk tradition as politically conservative, most Americans associate folk with "subversive" and radical activities—especially since the McCarthyite attacks on folksingers during the 1950s.

Current approaches to folk song move along the same lines. In 1954, the International Folk Music Council offered a definition of folk music that is still widely accepted:

> Folk music is the product of a musical tradition that has been evolved through the process of oral transmission. The factors that shape the tradition are: (i) continuity which links the present with the past; (ii) variation which springs from the creative impulse of the individual or the group; and (iii) selection by the community which determines the form or forms in which the music survives.
>
> The term can be applied to music that has been evolved from rudimentary beginnings by a community uninfluenced by popular and art music and it can likewise be applied to music which has

14

originated with an individual composer and has subsequently been absorbed into the unwritten living tradition of a community.

The term does not cover composed popular music that has been taken over ready-made by a community and remains unchanged, for it is the refashioning and recreation of the music by the community that gives it its folk character.[9]

This Darwinian definition, with its use of such terms as continuity, selection, and variation, makes suspect any materials that are written down in any form, not only by a composer (who then becomes a known author) but also by the anonymous or corporate publishers of broadsides and of collections in pamphlets or books. The definition implies illiteracy and a totally oral-oriented society. The preference for traditions "evolved from rudimentary beginnings" applies clearly to tribal cultures that have not been influenced by "popular" or "art" music. It is hard to say what parameters such a conception sets on what folk is or can be, but it would appear to eliminate most of western culture as well as the developed societies of the New World. Early Native American tribal cultures would fit quite well, if they were taken into account; African-American traditions obviously would not.

While such views seem to accommodate contemporaneity by suggesting that a composed work might become folk through an evolutionary process of absorption and presumably stylistic change by the folk, they still posit that folk expression can only emerge from a long, slow procedure during which the homogeneous preferences of a tribal folk are in command. The preference for homogeneity is another obvious and special problem for folklore in American culture. Although Americans have persistently resisted the notion of pluralism in general, the fact of multiculturalism is inarguable. In fact, the idea of multiculturalism has been widely acknowledged only since the "roots phenomenon" that followed the publication of Alex Haley's book and the television series based on it.[10]

Other folklorists have identified different features that purportedly distinguish folk songs from other sorts of music. Jeff Todd Titon has offered one that focuses on the performance aspects of different traditions.

An earlier generation of folklorists considered folksong to be a separate entity, distinct from popular music (associated with professional entertainers, the profit motive, and mass media) and from classical music (associated with elite groups, written musical scores, and unvarying performances). Folksongs were defined as traditional music that passed by ear and imitation from one singer or instrumentalist to the next, changing words and tunes as they went and, over time, giving the music the stamp of the community; the age and folk-quality of a folksong could be determined from the multiple versions collected. Folksongs were understood to flourish in rural, preindustrial areas among an illiterate peasantry; literacy, industrialization, and urbanization were regarded as enemies of folk traditions. This definition, while useful, could not account for folksong's persistence among close-knit ethnic groups in modern cities; it also placed undue emphasis on the idea that folksong was a text with a tune. . . . Folklorists today conceive of a folksong as a performance, not an item; its meaning and folk quality arises from what it communicates in the performance situation. . . . Popular music differs from folksong because it detaches its audience from the performance. This raised platform of the concert stage symbolizes the separation of performer and audience, as does the acoustically isolated musician's booth in the recording studios, where producers and engineers quite literally manufacture popular music from interchangeable parts. The audience buys popular music as a commodity, whether on record or in concert. Popular music is a product to consume. Folk music is an event to share.[11]

But folk song performance always distances artists from audiences, even if the space is a back porch and a seat below. And anyone who has ever attended a rock concert can testify that it is often a fully shared event.

Scholars have had an equally difficult time dealing with folk instruments such as the five-string banjo and the Appalachian three-string dulcimer, which are uniquely American developments and defy the notion that there is no strictly American folk tradition. Along with such instruments as the autoharp (a chorded zither reinvented around the turn of the century) and the folk harmonica (or blues-harp, a staple of current pop music styles), these musical developments are of major significance in our understanding of folk and pop movements, but they are rarely discussed by academics.

Another approach to defining what folk is simply categorizes the areas of interest to folklorists without articulating what features they share. Richard M. Dorson, perhaps the most influential folklorist of our time, has defined folklore as "both a field of learning and the whole subject matter of that field." Folk materials can be placed in four categories. The first is oral literature and includes "spoken, sung, and voiced forms of traditional utterance that show repetitive patterns." A second is "physical folklife, generally called material culture," defined to include "techniques, skills, recipes, and formulas transmitted across generations and subject to the same forces of conservative tradition and individual variation as verbal art." Folklorists examine the material culture of "high civilization" for evidences of "cultural lag" from "older submerged culture."

A third area is what Dorson has termed "social folk custom," or "group interaction rather than . . . individual skills and performance." This area, often otherwise defined as folk beliefs or custom and usage, deals with community traditions, rites of passage, and the many forms of activity characteristic of human behavior, including folk medicine and folk religion. Folk religion, according to Dorson, includes "folk reinterpretations of Christian doctrine and gospel, as in American Negro revisions of Baptist services through the incantatory sermon and congregational spiritual."

Dorson's fourth category of folk expression is "the performing arts," which refers to "traditional music, dance, and drama." This is a particularly confusing group of materials, not as "casual" as the rendition of a folktale and folk song and sometimes intersecting with the "formal performing arts" and elements of "high culture [which] continually seep into folk repertoires."[12]

Dorson's system, while a convenient typology for the folklorist, has little connection with the actual life of the folk, who rarely specialize in a particular mode of expression: in the field, one quite regularly finds a banjo picker who is also a fiddler and storyteller and perhaps a craftsperson as well. Dorson's schema, developed largely for those who are trained in verbal lore and not in musical traditions, masks the unity and integrity of folk expression.

For his part, Henry Glassie has emphasized Dorson's point about the distinction between individual and collective creativity. "Folklore, existentially, is the unification of the creative individual

17

with the collective through mutual action," Glassie has declared, as well as the symbol and celebration of "the willing submission of individuals to their own cultures."[13]

Folklorists still talk around their subject and steer away from precise definitions. In his address celebrating "the imperishable human spirit" before the California Folklore Society, William A. Wilson argued open-mindedly that "we folklorists must contribute to this effort by broadening prevailing concepts of the humanities, and of literature in particular . . . and by persuading our friends in other disciplines and among the general public to seek evidence of the significance of human life, not just in those canonized masterworks taught in our own literature classes but in works of our own invention and in our own capacity to create and appreciate beauty."[14] But Wilson did not suggest in any specific terms how folklore might be "broadened." Nor did any of the contributors to a 1991 issue of *Western Folklore* that proposed to take stock of the present and future of folklore studies. Robert A. Georges argued against colleagues who have taken folklore to be "whatever folklorists are interested in" or "those things that folklorists care to talk about," and he expressed dismay that folklorists often simply give themselves the title without any legitimate training in the field. On the other hand, Georges remarked with some concern of how often folklorists hesitate to give themselves the title, preferring to ground themselves in more traditional fields. For Georges, the solution is clear: "The right to identify oneself as a folklorist should be earned, and formal academic training is the way to earn that right. Those in charge of the training must themselves be academically trained, and they must see to it that those whom they teach are trained to become folklorists, *not* Americanists, anthropologists, linguists, museologists, musicologists, oral historians, organizational behaviorists, socio-linguists, or anything else." Georges concluded by expressing the hope that Dorson's early dream of a Ph.D. in folklore would someday be fully realized.[15]

In the same issue, Jay Mechling, whose background is in American studies, recommended that folklorists would do well to become knowledgeable in communication studies, as he has himself. And, in a response to the articles in this special issue, Elliot Oring argued that despite the fact that "almost everyone seems to agree that something is *wrong* with folklore and that the future of folklore studies in the United States depends on something being fixed or otherwise improved," the field's progress in recent years makes one wonder what would have happened if folklorists had gotten everything right.[16]

Folklorists who have consistently gone beyond these limited categories and assumptions are few, but they do exist. Alan Dundes, for example, has argued that folklore should not be identified exclusively with "peasant society or rural groups. . . . An equally fallacious view is that folklore was produced by a folk in the hoary past and the folklore still extant today consists of fragmentary survivals—what Dorson has called 'submerged culture.' " For Dundes, folk "can refer to *any group of people whatsoever* who share at least one common factor. It does not matter what the linking factor is—it could be a common occupation, language, or religion—but what is important is that a group formed for whatever reason will have some traditions which it calls its own."[17] Dundes has suggested that an itemized list of the forms of folklore, rather than a taxonomy, might be a convenient way of approaching the subject. In his view, such a list would include myth as well as envelope sealing and holiday customs.

Despite his unrelenting orthodox Freudianism, no one has done more than Dundes to show the persistence and the vitality of folk tradition in the modern world. His studies of jokes, the lore of offices and business, the material of sports and other group activities, and "latrinalia" (bathroom graffiti) have demonstrated beyond question that the folk still create in modern societies. But while he is correct in emphasizing that folklore is the result of a group process—a tribe, a Boy Scout troop, a union, or a Rotary club—Dundes also fails to offer a statement about the fundamental sources of this activity.[18]

Still, despite forays into modern materials by such "conservative" folklorists as Brunvand,[19] most scholars are content to accept the assumptions established a century ago, in part because a fundamental question that resists definition rests beneath the study of folklore (as of matter). Like physicists, folklorists are confounded partly because they try to fathom and hypostatize the precise nature of a basic natural function, in this case the human imagination.

And just as the attempt to locate fundamental essences of matter diffuses the material under inspection itself, so also the attempt to capture the substance of the creative process is defeated by the protean nature of its being. Facing these problems, folklorists often defeat their purposes through their own rhetoric, as in the following example by an otherwise capable and experienced critic: "The manifest works we traditionally associate with culture are not identical to the ethnonoetic *plenum*, the culture, which ethnomimesis generates and sustains, any more than a mathematical equation is identical to the truth which it expresses, even though that truth may not be accessible, or communicable, except through the equation. Hence through ethnomimesis the content of culture—its unconscious codes and impalpable images as well as its manifest works—replicates and modifies itself within the community and migrates across the boundary of one community and another to become, though transfigured by its new environment, an element in the life of adjacent cultures."[20]

*Folklore and the folk process reveal the ordinary and basic modes of human creativity,* a phenomenon that is physical, mental, and chemical. Creativity is the very locus of human energy and is indefinable in any form. The effort to define folklore is complicated by the fact that folklorists have become accustomed to undervaluing the accomplishments of ordinary people, preferring rather to believe that only the special geniuses express true creativity. As Claude Lévi-Strauss has shown, such an assumption does not mirror historical reality:

> It was in neolithic times that man's mastery of the great arts of civilization—of pottery, weaving, agriculture and the domestication of animals—became firmly established. No one today would any longer think of attributing these enormous advances to the fortuitous accumulation of a series of chance discoveries or believe them to have been revealed by the passive perception of certain natural phenomena. . . . To transform a weed into a cultivated plant, a wild beast into a domestic animal, to produce, in either of these, nutritious or technological useful properties which were originally absent or could only be guessed at; to make stout water-tight pottery out of clay which is friable and unstable, liable to pulverize or crack (which, however, is possible only if from a large number of organic and inorganic materials, the one most suitable for refining is se-

lected, and also the appropriate fuel, the temperature and duration of firing and the effective degree of oxidation); to work out techniques, often long and complex, which permit cultivation without soil or alternately without water; to change toxic roots or seeds into foodstuffs or again to use their poison for hunting, war or ritual—there is no doubt that all these achievements required a genuinely scientific attitude, sustained and watchful interest and a desire for knowledge for its own sake. For only a small proportion of observations and experiments (which must be assumed to have been primarily inspired by a desire for knowledge) could have yielded practical and immediately useful results. There is no need to dwell on the working of bronze and iron and of precious metals or even the simple working of copper ore by hammering which preceded metallurgy by several thousand years, and even at that stage they all demand a very high level of technical proficiency.[21]

Lévi-Strauss is trying to show that the major inventions that define civilization are the result of the same quality of mind that characterizes contemporary humanity. He argues that "Neolithic, or early historical, man was therefore the heir of a long scientific tradition." That is to say, the remarkable achievements of early humanity reveal most clearly the basic creativity that defines our species; we should not be surprised that even "primitive" societies are capable of extremely sophisticated mental activity. The difference between the early scientific achievements of humankind and more recent developments, Lévi-Strauss argued, was not the result of two different kinds of mentality but rather two different "strategic levels" of the same human mind.

Lévi-Strauss's argument bears emphasis because it substantiates the notion that ordinary human creativity was not only the source of humanity's basic accomplishments but continues to be so to the present time. As the more abstract qualities of creativity settled into the domain of modern science, the folk process came to be identified as an essential foundation of the creative power that has always provided special insights and unique artistic creations. The notion that folk implies antiquity and historically remote occasions is thus a major fallacy of much thought about folklore.[22]

As William F. H. Nicolaisen has pointed out, "Tradition, the key ingredient in so much folk cultural activity, has been equated with communal creation and re-creation in an atmosphere of anonymity, and the emphasis has been on the transmission of knowledge, customs, and beliefs through such channels in an almost mystical fashion."[23] This comment should remind us that the term traditional has many different meanings. It does often imply the idea of antiquity, but traditional also refers to an older mode of transmitting information and techniques, directly from mouth to mouth and hand to hand. African drummers sometimes take their students' hands in their own to transmit the beat, just as contemporary teachers of violin often place their students' fingers on the correct place on the fingerboard. Both examples of traditional folk processes illustrate that some things can only be transmitted directly in this fashion and often resist written modes of explanation such as musical notation or other indirect instruction.

Tradition also implies the notion of balance between individual and collective expression. As recent literary criticism has argued, all texts are related; we can never describe any one as unique. While the intertextualism these critics espouse may occasionally become extreme,[24] it is a good corrective for the idea of unbridled individualism and helps to underscore the common heritage of language.[25] The connections are not simple, but traditional is the term that prompts us to remember the crucial involvements of what Whitman liked to call the "I and the en-masse." It brings to mind what I call imaginary anthropology, an idea which shows up in the work of many seminal thinkers, including Locke, Marx, Freud, and T. S. Eliot: in a state of nature, the theory goes, the individual and the group were in perfect balance. But after the fall (due to varieties of original sinning) the balance is undone. We are left in our current state of disequilibrium, and tradition is the trace of that primitive moment.

Our modern condition remains unbalanced, and the age tends to overemphasize the function of individualism. Arguments about our original condition, as Jacques Derrida has pointed out, are attempts to suppress the notion of "primordial difference" and perpetuate the myth of perfection in the state of nature. Regardless of how we deal with this illusion, we must not become victims of elitist arguments that overlook the continuing power of the folk imagination. And we should not be limited by an educational sys-

tem that generally maintains creativity is the province of a select
group of highly individual professionals whose powers we can ad-
mire but rarely emulate. The American folk tradition does not in-
volve the "submission" of individuals to culture, as Glassie has
suggested; rather, creative individuals use folk styles to make major changes in cultural materials. Herder's assertion of this point is
what made his work so interesting to such American writers as
Emerson, Whitman, Constance Rourke, and Alan Lomax, all deeply
committed to democratic ideology.

Still, the work of most of the influential folklorists of our time has
been weighted toward the force of tradition not so much because
the concept seemed to correct extreme individualism but because
it underscores the anonymity of "authentic" folk expression. But as
Richard Bauman has noted, new thinking about folklore over the
past twenty years has tended to turn away from viewing the folk as
an "anonymous collectivity" and to focus more on "the individual
performer."[26] The presence of identifiable sources (in song and
lore) has always been a major aspect of American folk development, but the unwillingness of folklorists to acknowledge them has
denied us an adequate definition of folk styles in our society. The
folk process, which has been seen as centering on the disappearance of the individual artist into a communal tradition, must be
reconceived to recognize the contribution of known individuals to
the folk legacy.

One of the greatest inventions of the folk is, in fact, language, the
foundation of all other types of folklore. As Walt Whitman insisted:
"Language, be it remembered, is not an abstract construction of
the learn'd, or of dictionary makers, but is something arising out of
the work, needs, ties, joys, affections, tastes, of long generations
of humanity, and has its bases broad and low, close to the ground.
Its final decisions are made by the masses, people nearest the concrete, having most to do with the actual land and sea. It imperme-
ates all, the Past as well as the Present, and it is the grandest
triumph of the human intellect."[27] Like Lévi-Strauss, Whitman asserted that the central human characteristic, symbolic expression,
is an ancient accomplishment of common people rather than the
invention of academics. In addition, he insisted that this feat was
not only historic but also contemporary.

Common sense verifies such arguments. Who has not seen children expressing themselves poetically, dancing freely, singing their own tunes, filling pages with intriguing illustrations? But it is equally true that after five or ten years of education, students cannot read or write effectively, cannot draw, and cringe at the thought that someone might ask them to sing or dance. Most Americans see these latter arts, among the elemental human capabilities, as cruel punishments when demanded in public.[28] It is amazing that the inherited skills of humanity can survive at all under a school regimen that persistently treats practice in the arts as a frill easily eliminated from the curriculum. The need to be creative then finds outlets in noneducational areas and in subjects never taught in schools—how to decorate a Volkswagen, for example, or paint a subway train. Not surprisingly, many of these expressions represent protest against a culture that finds no acceptable place for ordinary human creativity.[29]

Although American culture often defines the behavior of "innocent" children as "romantic" excess, ordinary adults as well as children possess creativity, and the ways in which they express it are folklore itself. So deeply imbedded in the nature of human beings, the essence of this attribute is difficult, perhaps impossible, to locate precisely—it is a kind of cultural indeterminacy principle. Although we see its effects more clearly in groups and associate it historically with variously organized societies, the underlying capability resides in each human being.[30] Whether its effects are encouraged or repressed depends on many factors, both personal and cultural. In societies where a democratic ideology informs the quality of the culture it is possible to appreciate how the folk contribute to the arts as well as the political ideology of a nation, outcomes that Herder and his followers in the United States first identified.

I am reminded of the colloquy between John Adams and Thomas Jefferson on a topic closely related to these issues. During the last years of their lives, Adams and Jefferson carried on a lengthy correspondence that continued in a chivalrous and carefully restrained form the basic disagreements they had experienced in their earlier political contacts. Adams confided in Jefferson his concerns that a democratic society such as that established in the United States could not develop sufficiently educated and virtuous individuals to serve in the government and implement effectively its commands. Aristocracies, he pointed out, have a long and well-defined tradition of training people for public service, a tradition notably lacking in the United States. "The five Pillars of Aristocracy," he explained, "are Beauty, Wealth, Birth, Genius and Virtues. Any one of the three first, can at any time over bear any one of the two last." Jefferson's affirmation of the power of the folk in his response to Adams's argument is one of the great justifications of a democratic ideology.

> For I agree with you that there is a natural aristocracy among men. The grounds of this are virtue and talents. . . . The natural aristocracy I consider as the most precious gift of nature for the instruction, the trusts, and government of society. And indeed it would have been inconsistent in creation to have formed man for the social state, and not to have provided virtue and wisdom enough to manage the concerns of the society. May we not even say that form of government is the best which provides the most effectually for a pure selection of the natural aristoi into the offices of government? . . . *You* think it best to put the Pseudo-aristoi into a separate chamber of legislation where they may be hindered from doing mischief by their coordinate branches, . . . *I* think the best remedy is exactly that provided by all our constitutions, to leave the citizens the free election and separation of the aristoi from the pseudo-aristoi, of the wheat from the chaff. In general they will elect the real good and wise. In some instances, wealth may corrupt, and birth blind them but not in sufficient degree to endanger the society.[31]

I think most Americans today would clearly side with Adams; it makes sense to believe that a better-trained, well-educated individual ought to be a more effective officeholder than a "natural aristocrat." But Jefferson proposed a characteristically radical view of ordinary people. He assumed that talent and virtue are distributed randomly in a population and do not arise from privilege and wealth. In a democratic society it should be possible for the people to identify these abilities wherever they appear instead of prejudging the locus of talent and virtue. Jefferson's abiding faith in the power of ordinary people can easily be extended to their capacity for artistic expression. Many people simply cannot believe that an untrained folk musician, for example, could have the ability and

25

sophistication of an academy-trained classical performer. But one has only to listen to the work of our great blues artists, fiddlers, and banjo pickers or to view the creations of craftsworkers in many fields to realize the flaw in such assumptions. The overwhelming power and technical virtuosity of many folk artists settle the controversy without question.[32]

The radicalism of Jefferson's thought is also an important element in our concerns with the nature of folk modes of creativity. As we have seen, the idea of conservatism figures prominently in the definitions of many academic folklorists, not only in the sense of retaining traditions but also in a political sense as well. When the idea of folk emerges in much intellectual discussion it is usually seen through the filter of a European and, according to my view, outdated attitude. Take for example the arguments of Cleanth Brooks, one of our most perceptive critics who often writes about the character of Southern literature and its preoccupation with the folk. When Brooks wants to talk about the nature of folk communities, he proposes to look at "the parallels between the cultures out of which Yeats and Faulkner came." He argues that "A vigorous folk culture implies a number of other parallel features—conservatism, old-fashioned customs and ideas, a paternalistic system centered in an aristocracy or at least a landowning squirearchy. In short, a folk society based on the land implies the Big House with landed proprietors and the ethos that goes with such a governing class as part of the larger cultural continuum in which the folk subsists."[33] Of course, Brooks is careful to note that "The particular details of the cultural situation as between Ireland and the Old South were, as we would expect, vastly different." The main difference, he notes, is that slavery mollified the class differences in the South because "In one sense, all the whites stood together despite the class barriers that existed within the white society." But despite the unique circumstances generated by the presence of slavery, Brooks is determined to stick with his definition of folk as conservative and aristocratic. Such conceptions simply do not apply to American culture. And this is especially true about black folk culture, which is notoriously not conservative or paternalistic, and is not involved with anything like an authentic aristocracy. Whatever may be the conditions in Yeats's folk culture, they do not apply to ours. Brooks is much closer to an important insight when he quotes Yeats's homage to folk diction: "I have spent my life in clearing out of poetry every phrase written for the eye, and bringing all back to syntax that is for ear alone." In other respects, however, Brooks epitomizes the approach toward the folk still espoused by most of our folklorists and critics who talk about the meaning of folk. Jefferson's notion of the natural aristocracy enables us to see a specific justification for democracy—the fact that the creative powers can be found everywhere in human nature; perhaps what we hold most in common is the fact that we are human and inherit the ability to use our creative faculties. This ordinary creativity is a continuous process in human culture, not old-fashioned, or aristocratic, or paternalistic. And in the United States as in no other nation, folk tradition has continually mixed materials, especially those from African-American and Anglo-American sources, but also many others from numerous ethnic traditions. America's most influential writers, from Emerson and Whitman to Faulkner and Ralph Ellison, have developed an esthetic that acknowledges the artistic power emanating from the folk, a concept whose roots lie in the eighteenth-century philosophy of Johann Gottfried Herder.

# TWO

## Herder and
## Folk Ideology

Although scholars still find it difficult to define folk, Herder was specific and consistent in his use of the term. In a rigidly stratified society like Herder's, the folk represented those segments of the population removed from formal education and the influence of the established arts—in eighteenth-century Germany, the peasantry. Herder shocked his contemporaries by insisting that this low class effectively germinated the nation's culture.

Johann Gottfried Herder was born in Mohrungen, East Prussia, on 25 August 1744. His father had followed the family trade of weaving but had been forced to give it up and become a schoolmaster in order to support his family. Herder's mother, Anna Elisabeth Pelz, was also born in Mohrungen and, like her husband, was extremely devout. After studying in the local Latin school, Herder was amanuensis to a town official until 1762 when he was offered an opportunity to study medicine in Königsberg, the provincial capital. An army surgeon stationed in the area with the Russian troops that had occupied East Prussia during the time of the Seven Years War was Herder's sponsor. In return for the opportunity to study at the medical school, Herder was to provide a Latin translation of a monograph the surgeon had written. Herder's medical career, however, was short-lived—he passed out during the first dissection in his anatomy class.

Although it meant the loss of his patron, Herder changed his course of study to theology, a vocation he followed throughout his life. At Königsberg, he had come under the influence of Immanuel

Kant and Johann Georg Hamann, two crucial figures in his intellectual life; later, at Strassburg, he met Goethe, with whom he had a lifelong association that waxed and waned as each pursued his own interests. Herder served in ecclesiastical posts in Riga, Bückeburg, and Weimar. In 1773 he married Caroline Flachsland, a sensitive and emotional woman with whom Herder enjoyed a full and satisfying relationship, together with their seven surviving children. On 18 December 1803, attended by his son Gottfried, a physician, Herder died in Weimar.

Herder was born almost at the midpoint of the Age of Reason, that moment in the history of European thought when the Enlightenment claimed to have illuminated the darkness of earlier epochs and raised humanity to its apex. At the same time, mass movements extolling a reawakening of religious enthusiasm were sweeping through England and the American colonies, harbingers of the major philosophical changes that were shortly to come.

Although the Enlightenment was in full sway during Herder's formative years, he was one of the last Renaissance men, a significant figure in philosophy, history, philology, sociology, biblical studies, and folklore. He is acknowledged as one of the founders (along with Giambattista Vico) of the philosophy of history; his speculations about the nature of the state made him a crucial figure in political science and sociology: his investigations of the origins of language foreshadowed even the most current linguistic research; and his interest in folklore and folk song changed the esthetic values of his contemporaries and continues to be relevant in modern folklore studies.

Herder developed these concerns amid his critique of Enlightenment rationalism. In his major work, *Ideen zur Philosophie der Geschichte der Menschheit (Outlines of a Philosophy of the History of Humankind),* published in four parts between 1784 and 1791, Herder took strong exception to the Enlightenment notion that human civilization was at its apogee. "It would be the most stupid vanity," he declared, "to imagine that all the inhabitants of the world must be Europeans to live happily." His criticism of rationalism provoked many in his own time and today to view Herder as a reactionary and backward-looking thinker or as an extreme nationalist and chauvinist. But Herder's antagonism to the Enlightenment was based on his awareness of its severe social, psycho-logical, and scientific limitations. According to Herder biographer Robert T. Clark, Jr., the attitude of Enlightenment thinkers toward the cultures of the past was conditioned by a "caste system in eighteenth-century anthropology." Only the cultures of Greece, Rome, and France were considered historically important, and any nation aspiring to become a "high" civilization had to imitate them. In practice the intelligentsia had to reject its own heritage and adapt the values of more prestigious societies. In Herder's time the literary tastes of the upper classes in Germany were drawn to the achievements of the French court and such formidable figures as Molière, Corneille, and Racine; the idea of a distinctly German liter-ature (in the barbaric German language) was unthinkable.[1]

Herder was especially disturbed by the arrogance of Enlight-enment thinkers who adopted uncritically the idea of progress—the notion that the present moment, because of its technologi-cal achievements, was by definition superior to earlier periods of history.[2] Enlightenment ideologues argued that cultural progress would be achieved only by dispelling myth and superstition from the minds of the peasantry and replacing them with the new light of rationalist philosophies. They believed it particularly important to erase any influences that might remain from the Middle Ages, viewed as a period of darkness in which religious oppression and an irrational folk tradition fostered antiscientific ideas. Only af-ter being liberated from this pernicious heritage could the lower orders of society be raised to the level of educated individuals. Obviously, this point of view rendered nationalistic movements ri-diculous and useless. High culture instead moved toward a univer-salized standard of behavior and values that left no room for eso-teric individual or regional expression. Rationalist philosophers thus placed their faith in the ability of rational thinkers to discover universal principles that would eliminate the peculiar qualities of individual groups. Herder's notion that each society has its own independent value and gains its national character from the cre-ative efforts of its peasantry was heretical by this standard.

Eighteenth-century Germany was not a nation at all. It consisted of almost two thousand discrete territories of varying size and political systems, each ruled by its own sovereign. The resulting economic disunity was aggravated by religious feuds and the aftermath of the Thirty Years War. Created amid these circumstances, Herder's work was permeated by one overriding concern—to discover the sources for the creation of a distinctly German literary tradition that would define the nature of an independent nation. Opposing the tendency of the Enlightenment to value general, universal characteristics, Herder sought to isolate the qualities that were unique to the German experience. But he was not interested in establishing a concept of racial superiority. As F. M. Barnard has noted of Herder's thought, "*Volk* was conceived as an ethnic and not a racial community. . . . What is more, the idea of racial superiority, which is the key concept of modern racialism, was completely alien to Herder's mind. He firmly rejected the notion of superman and the idea of master-nations or master-races. Domination or persecution of any kind, whether of man by man, or of one nation by another, was abhorrent to his very being."[3] Clark has argued similarly: "Both Herder and Goethe, in preaching a revival of interest in German poetry and architecture, were completely internationalistic in their outlook. . . . The idea of race, of course, was utterly foreign to their thought. Illustrative of this broad tolerance of outlook is the variety of folk songs of all nations used by Herder to impress upon the Germans the need of gathering and preserving their own folk heritage."[4]

In fact, Herder questioned the conception of race itself, a position that Kant (in his review of the *Ideen*) criticized severely. Though some thinkers used the term race "for four or five divisions, according to the regions of origin or complexion," Herder saw no value in the term. He notes that "every distinct community is a *nation,* having its own national culture as it has its own language. The climate, it is true, may imprint on each its peculiar stamp, or it may spread over it a slight veil, without destroying, however, its original national character. . . . In short, there are neither four or five races, nor exclusive varieties on the earth. Complexions run into each other: forms follow the genetic character: and *in toto* they are, in their final analysis, but different shades of the same great picture which extends through all ages and all parts of the earth. Their study, therefore, properly forms no part of biology or systematic natural history, but belongs rather to the anthropological history of man."[5]

As if to underscore the international implications of his proposals, Herder's first collection of *Volkslieder (Folksongs)*, published in 1778, contained not only German material but examples from Italian, Estonian, Lithuanian, Lettish, Danish, Spanish, Inca, Eskimo, Latin, Greek, and Old Norse. The methodology is far from satisfying the standards of contemporary folklore or anthropological research, yet the work stands as a major instance of the internationalism of Herder's thought, and, Clark has argued, it was the inspiration for the folklore movement of the nineteenth century. "The new realm of poetic reference opened by the *Folk Songs* effectively distracted really gifted poets from the fatuous adherence to a narrowly limited set of foreign cultural models," Clark has observed. "In the final balance, then, Herder's *Folk Songs* contributed to the building of a national German literature. After that development, it is true, this literary nationalism went to excess; but it would be absurd to attribute that phase to Herder's warmly humane, honestly and tolerantly national striving."[6]

Herder began formulating his ideas about folk expression after reading Bishop Thomas Percy's *Reliques of Ancient English Poetry* (1765), although he was skeptical of the ideas that guided Percy's collecting impulse. Though not the first investigation of the English folk song tradition, Percy's collection was a great influence on the neoclassic as well as the pre-Romantic scholars and folklorists of the period. The ballads and songs in the *Reliques,* Percy wrote, were "rude survivals of the past, deserving of a certain amount of attention as illustrating the language, the numbers, the beliefs and customs of bygone days, although as poetry they had no intrinsic value."[7]

Almost from the beginning of modern interest in folk songs, then, the seeds of antiquarianism were sown. Examples of folk expression were viewed only as remnants from the past, artifacts of bygone cultures, and their significance for the scholar lay in the glimpses they provided into the mores and attitudes of "primitive" or unenlightened peoples. It followed also that folk songs underscored the immense gap between the clumsy poetry of the folk and the polished verse of sophisticated writers. In this respect, too, Percy was a precursor of many later collectors and folklorists who also would not consider folk poetry comparable with the accomplishments of "civilized" writers. Although there were some notable exceptions, Herder included, folklorists in Percy's time and thereafter shared his view that folk song was quaint, curious, and of some historical or philosophical interest; it was essentially a thing of the past, a kind of literary fossil that, considering its low social origins, was clearly inferior to formal verse.

Unlike Percy and most other scholars of the time, Herder expressed no condescension toward folk song and its creators. In a comment that foreshadows Ralph Waldo Emerson's view in *The American Scholar,* he instead deplored the tendency to dismiss such expression: "In more than one province I know of folksongs, songs in dialect, peasant songs which as regards vivacity, and rhythm, simplicity and strength of language, would certainly concede nothing to many of those collected by other nationalities. But who would collect them? Who would trouble himself about the songs of the people on the streets, in alleys and fish markets, in the simple roundelay of the peasant folk, about songs which are often without scansion and with bad rhymes? . . . We would rather read, even though only for pastime, our modern beautifully printed poets."[8]

For Herder, the existence of a vital folk tradition was significant primarily not for the light it could throw on the nature of ancient civilizations. On the contrary, Herder believed that a nation's formal literature needed to be based on the creative accomplishments of its folk, regardless of how crude that body of materials may seem to sophisticated classes of society. A national literature thus conceived, he argued, would be the basis for a uniquely developed nation that would see no need to imitate the attitudes or values of any other culture. From the viewpoint of Enlightenment thinkers, as well as the orthodox religious establishment, Herder's notions were patently ridiculous, for he had turned the prestige ladder of society upside down. It had always been assumed that an aristocratic or middle-class elite created the cultural and political values of a people; these ideas then percolated down to the lower classes who retained these corrupted traditions. Herder maintained that the masses created a culture's basic values; the upper classes later refined those essential materials, and in the process diminished their vitality.

Almost from the first, Herder turned his attention to language because the ability to symbolize is a determining quality of what it means to be human. As F. M. Barnard noted, "It was not blood but language which Herder regarded as the essential criterion of a *Volk*."[9] Herder was struck by the tendency among German writers to use Latin or French and to avoid using German in their work. The elite had despised German as a barbaric dialect good for "miners and hunters" but not for sophisticated intellects. Herder was the first to admit that the German language "can unquestionably learn from others in which one thing or another can be better expressed . . . it might learn from Greek simplicity and dignity of expression, from Latin the Golden mean of nicety, from English brief fullness, from French gay liveliness, and from Italian soft picturesque-ness. However, no genius need be ashamed of his mother tongue, or make complaints of it; because for every excellent writer ideas are the sons of heaven, words the daughters of earth."[10] If writers could stay close to the folk sources of their own language, in other words, they could develop their own genius and at the same time express the values of the culture. Herder in fact argued that a nationality without a language of its own is impossible. "Know your own language . . . and develop it for poetry and prose," he advised the writers of his time. "For then you are building the foundation that will hold a building."[11] Because of the impact of the Renaissance and the Enlightenment, the domination of Latin over the German language, and the subservience of German writers to French literary traditions, Herder believed that Germany had been kept from tapping the roots of its own culture:

> From ancient times we have absolutely no living poetry on which our newer poetry might grow like a branch on the stem. Other nationalities have progressed with the centuries and built with national products upon a peculiar foundation, with the remnants of the past on the belief and tastes of the *Volk*. In that way their literature and language have become national. The voice of the *Volk* is used and cherished, and in these matters they have cultivated a much larger public than we have. . . . It will remain eternally true that if we have no *Volk*, we

34

shall have no public, no literature of our own which shall live and work in us. Unless our literature is founded on our *Volk*, we shall write eternally for closet sages or disgusting critics out of whose mouths and stomachs we shall get back what we have given.[12]

Herder was aware of the fact that language is created not by writers or the editors of dictionaries but by the uses and needs of ordinary people. He realized that idioms, those peculiar figurative expressions in a language, are the elements that provide its special character and distinguish it absolutely from other languages: "The idioms are the elegances of which no neighbor can deprive us and they are sacred to the tutelary goddess of the language. They are the elegances woven into the spirit of the language, and this spirit is destroyed if they are taken out. . . . The idioms [of our early writers] should be collected. . . . And if they are good for nothing else they will at least open the way to the student of language so he can understand the genius of the nationality and explain one by the other. The idioms of every language are the impressions of its country, its nationality, its history."[13] To Herder, idioms stood in the same relationship to language as the folk songs did to formal literature: they provide the vitality and spirit that distinguish truly national expression. Each language is unique through the working of its idioms, but all languages are equal in their ability to create them. There are, in other words, no poor languages. Herder presaged contemporary linguistic approaches in recognizing that even the least "civilized" culture may be as rich (or richer) in its linguistic resources than nations more materially developed. At the same time he recognized the crucial function of language: without it, he insisted, we cannot even think, because our intellectual processes only take place through the medium of words.

Herder's essentially organic views of language and folk tradition symbolize a major turn from the materialist and mechanistic conceptions of Newton and other Enlightenment thinkers. Herder thus described the main route away from eighteenth-century neoclassicism toward the Romantic positions of the nineteenth century. In sociological terms, Herder's folk ideology implied that a society was not simply an undifferentiated whole but rather consisted of a dominant culture and an assortment of subcultures. Folk song is the product of a subculture that exists contemporaneously with the dominant culture rather than in a distant past. The idea that a subculture might not only contribute to the dominant one but actually define its major outlines remains a startling conception. At the same time, Herder's formulation marks him not only as unantiquarian but also as in fundamental disagreement with Rousseau. Rousseau emphasized the value of "primitive" cultures but asserted that civilization destroys them. Like Percy, he encouraged antiquarianism and nostalgia for some irretrievable golden age—an imaginary anthropology. By contrast, to Herder each historical moment had equal integrity, and the idea of progress had no relevance. Folk song was not to him the remnant of an antique and outmoded system of expression and values; it lives in contemporary society and speaks directly to the needs of women and men in their contemporary circumstances.

Herder developed, in fact, a principle of historical relativism that clearly prefigures modern anthropological methodology. He asserted that human expression began through song, and thus even the earliest ancestors of humankind were esthetically competent:

> Nature has conferred another beneficent gift on our species, in leaving to such of its members as are least stored with ideas the first gems of superior sense, exhilarating music. . . . and among the most uncultivated nations music is the first of the fine arts, by which every mind is moved. . . . But music, however rude and simple, speaks to every human heart, and this with the dance, constitutes Nature's general festival throughout the earth. Pity it is that most travellers, from too refined a taste, conceal from us those infantile tones of foreign nations. Useless as they may be to the musician, they are instructive to the investigators of man; for the music of a nation, in its most imperfect form and favourite tunes, displays the internal character of the people."[14]

Herder's assertion that folk song is the main source of literary value was met with derision and, in religious circles, with charges of blasphemy. One clerical critic, for example, complained that Herder's theoretical principles were being drawn from folk songs rather than Christian documents. Noting the condescension applied to the term *Volk* in his time, Herder suggested that in fact earlier cultures, particularly, as he perceived it, ancient Greece, understood the true meaning of the term. "There," he pointed out, "this name was honorable; it included all citizens except members of the council of priests; now it is synonymous with rabble and *canaille*. There all citizens were equal."[15] In fact, Herder argued, "A folk singer does not have to be from the rabble and sing for the rabble; just as little is the noblest poetry harmed by being sung by the people."[16] On the contrary, according to Herder, it is the folk bard who brings a truly national literature into existence. Although each nation's folk heritage guarantees it a unique and authentic expression, Herder also argued that folk poetry is valuable because of its "constant and international elements."

Like other German-speaking writers of the time, Herder used the term *Humanität* to describe the ultimate moment of individual and social development. It is a difficult word to render in English because it encompasses many elements; in part, according to Isaiah Berlin, it means "the harmonious development of all immortal souls toward universally valid goals; reason, freedom, toleration, mutual love and respect between individuals and societies, as well as physical and spiritual health, finer perceptions, dominion over the earth, the harmonious realization of all that God has implanted in His noblest work and made in His own image."[17] It has also been defined as a state of perfection in the sense that humanity would become what it was capable of, morally and ethically. In another sense it contained Herder's vision of the ultimate accomplishment of the values associated with Christian doctrines, a foreshadowing, perhaps, of the millennium. Clearly, *Humanität* as an idea of perfection carried no connotation of a "superman," but rather the notion of a completely and fully developed human being.

The radicalism of Herder's thought is best illustrated in his description of how *Humanität* may be achieved. He proposed that humanity passes through three stages, but not in a progressive or linear movement; rather, the process occurs independently for each individual society. No individual society can retrace its own history, which, like a footstep on the shore of an ocean, is quickly erased by the shifting tides. At the same time, every group that exists is capable of achieving *Humanität*. All development was thus equal and not literally comparable to any other.

The first stage involves the identification and acceptance of the folk tradition unique to each group and the corresponding rejection of the influence of all foreign cultures. For all social groups, finding one's roots is the necessary prelude to the second stage in Herder's framework—defining the outline of an indigenous culture and thereupon assuring national independence. Because it has been constructed on folk roots, the resulting national status will be unique and equal to all others that have existed or ever will exist. In theory, a nation so developed will have no need to threaten its neighbors, for it will be secure in its identity. Its cultural viability is measured in how closely its folk sources have been relied upon to construct literary as well as other artistic expression. This esthetic was completely opposed to that of the Enlightenment, which encouraged the formation of universal principles and an approach to language that moved further and further from "vulgar" folk usage.

Precisely how the national writers are to employ their folk sources is a matter of some significance. During the last part of the eighteenth century when the energy of the Enlightenment and its neoclassical style began to wane, writers in England and on the continent began to turn to folk materials, especially the dramatic-narrative songs called ballads. Even Goethe, who claimed his experiences with Herder were the most important in his life, thought that the lesson of Herder should lead poets to compose literary ballads, that is, imitate folk materials directly. Herder had turned Goethe from frivolous dilettantism toward a concern for the important issues of German culture during Goethe's years at Strassburg, where he had been sent to finish a law degree. "Herder's greatest contribution to Goethe was a way of looking at the entire process of art production, in the individual and society—both inseparable in Herder's conception of human life," Clark has noted. "It is fundamentally a new psychology (in the broadest sense of the word). . . . Interest in folk poetry, a just appreciation of such historical periods as the despised Middle Ages, assertion of the equal rights of all cultures—all these important attitudes are corollary to the main proposition, namely, that the individual human personality is unique and irreplaceable, existing in a specific time and space, interacting with an environment which itself changes as the individual develops."[18]

Goethe became a leading figure in the pre-Romantic period known as *Sturm und Drang* (Storm and Stress), which became the rubric for the entire Romantic movement in Germany (the term derives from the subtitle of a drama by Friedrich Maximilian von Klinger, published in 1776).[19] But he misunderstood Herder's ideas about how folk sources were to be used in literature, and indeed this misconception was widely spread during the Romantic period and has persisted in our own time. The touchstone of Herder's thought was to avoid imitation of any kind; folk materials provide an ideological connection rather than a model for literal emulation.

Goethe ultimately understood Herder's teaching when he went on to create his great work in its spirit rather than in an unimaginative interpretation of the theory. T. S. Eliot also apprehended that all great national writers, whose work contains "a strong local flavour combined with unconscious universality," are inherently regional as well as universal:

> When we read a novel of Dostoevski, or see a play by Tchehov [Chekhov], for the first time, I think we are fascinated by the odd way in which Russians behave; later we come to recognize that theirs is merely an odd way of expressing thoughts and feelings which we all share. And though it is only too easy for a writer to be local without being universal, I doubt whether a poet or novelist can be universal without being local too. Who could be more Greek than Odysseus? Or more German than Faust? Or more Spanish than Don Quixote? Or more American than Huck Finn? Yet each one of them is a kind of archetype in the mythology of all men everywhere.[20]

For Herder and for Eliot, creators of a national literature evoke their culture's values at the same time that they express their individual talents. Robert Frost described the process a little more precisely— "the beginning of literary form is in some turn given to the sentence in folk speech."[21] Herder was the first to describe this crucial relationship between artists and their most influential sources.

In Herder's third stage, the values of *Humanität* are achieved. Essentially, this third stage is international; Herder's program moves societies from folk to a national and ultimately to an international level. The folk period itself is international in the sense that every tribal culture has a folk tradition; similarly, while each nation will develop inimitably from its folk roots, the process is universal: it will be enacted by all peoples. To some critics the idea of a people's movement through three stages (which seems a characteristic

German equation) has suggested something akin to the Enlightenment's conception of the idea of progress, or even something comparable to the stages of Hegel's or Marx's philosophical systems. But to Herder, the idea of movement is advance to internationalism rather than progress toward a kind of supernationalism. The folk stage is no less valuable than the succeeding two; in fact, Herder viewed it as in some respects more vital. The folk experience is essentially oral (and aural), a condition that fosters an impressive flexibility and facility. Like later folklorists, Herder was overwhelmed by the power of bardic tradition, including that of Homer and "Ossian." The tales of Ossian, a legendary Celtic bard said to have flourished in the third century A.D., were preserved in Ireland and Scotland. James Macpherson claimed falsely to have discovered texts written by the bard himself. Even when Herder became convinced that the "Ossianic" poems of Macpherson were frauds, he was still impressed by the Scotsman's sensitivity to oral tradition and his ability to use Celtic materials so effectively. Herder believed no written work could equal the force of oral tradition.

According to Berlin, Herder felt that words, "by connecting passions with things, the present with the past, and by making possible memory and imagination, create family, society, literature, history. Herder declared that to speak and think in words is to 'swim in an inherited stream of words; we must accept these media on trust; we cannot create them.'" Language is thus a legacy that the sophisticated members of a society inherit from the folk, a source they do not always acknowledge. But if language alone makes it possible to conceptualize experience, in its written form it also freezes it. In that respect, Herder understood the advent of written language as a diminution of human expression. Oral tradition provides a constant pressure against what Herder called "linguistic petrification." Berlin has argued that the "history of linguistic revolutions is the history of the succession of cultures, the true revolutions in the history of the human race." Primitive poetry is essentially "magical and a spur to action—to heroes, hunters, lovers; it stimulates and directs. It is not to be savoured by the scholar in his armchair, but it is intelligible only to those who have placed themselves in situations similar to the conditions in which words sprang into existence."[22]

40

Herder saw the knowledge of a group's historical identity as essential to its survival: "to avert dispersion," he wrote, "they will do everything to strengthen their tribal roots." As Barnard has observed, this strengthening did not in Herder's view mean that groups would "adopt warlike postures, but rather that they will seek to maintain their sense of collective identity by treasuring and perpetuating the memory of a common past and all that this entails. They will extol the deeds of their forefathers, observe tribal customs and rituals and, above all, preserve the distinctness of their own language."[23]

Herder's position allowed him to see the virtues of earlier periods in human development without falling into a Rousseauistic yearning for a lost golden age. *Vom Geist der ebräischen Poesie (The Spirit of Hebrew Poetry),* published in two parts in 1782 and 1783, is an example of how carefully Herder could balance his evaluations of the past and present. It was translated into French and Dutch and became known among readers of English in the translation by James Marsh, published in 1833 when he was president of the University of Vermont. In his introduction, Marsh emphasized the value Herder placed on the need to appreciate the variety of national cultures:

> The more thoroughly one's understanding is moulded by the forms, and occupied with the conceptions exhibited in the literature of one age and country, the less is it qualified to imbibe the genuine spirit, and feel the simple power of every other national literature.... [One] must learn to place himself entirely in their *point of view,* and to see all these particulars in the relation to each other, and to the observer, which they would then assume. When he has done this, he will be prepared to understand why they thought and felt, and wrote as they did; and if he have the feeling and inspiration of the poet, he will sympathize with their emotions, and the living spirit of their poetry will be kindled up in his imagination.[24]

As Marsh realized, Herder saw the Hebrew Bible as essentially a work of poetry, a national poem built upon the earlier folk tradition of the Jews that, like Homer's writing, emerged at a society's second stage. For Herder, the importance of these Scriptures was not as dogma and doctrine but rather as "inspiration," the creative spark that kindles the imagination. In many respects these attitudes are the central clues to an emerging Romantic vision that Herder was among the first to comprehend. If the Scriptures are the inspired words of God, then Herder wanted them literally to make us all creative beings in the image of the deity. "When I hear in learned commentaries and paraphrases or even in the pulpit, much talk about imagery that must be translated into good, pure, intelligible German, that is, into metaphysical, abstract German, then I often do not know what to do," Herder wrote. "The former [metaphorical] language is understood by everyone; that latter is understood by no one."[25] Ultimately, Herder's view is that poetry and religion are one. Nothing could have been more shocking to Enlightenment thinkers or fundamentalist clerics. In what others saw as the barbarism of the ancient Jews, Herder found an impressive and moving poetic legacy that epitomized their national literature.

In the international stage, Herder did not expect these national sensibilities to wither away. He did not envision, as Marx later did, a monolithic socialism, communism, or any other absolutism. Barnard has asserted that for Herder *Humanität* was "a loose and informal linking of autonomous and co-operating nations. . . . This ultimate stage was to witness the disappearance of the state as an administrative machine, and its replacement by a pluralist diffusion of government associated with Herder's concept of 'nomocracy,' under which spontaneous 'joint effort' and 'self-determination' would dispense with violence and coercion."[26]

For Herder, tradition linked individual and collective identity. As Barnard has explained, Herder conceived tradition to be "not an accumulated *stock* of a set number of beliefs, customs and ways of doing things, but an ongoing *process* which by its very nature (as Herder describes it) entails the continuous merging of the old and new." This process from generation to generation involves both adapting tradition and evaluating it and thus, as Barnard has observed, "necessarily entails a certain dialectic in its operation." Language is the medium through which tradition in large part is passed, as Barnard has described:

> It unites [man] with, but it also differentiates him from others. Imperceptibly it also links him with the past. By means of language he is able to enter into communion with the way of thinking and feeling of

his progenitors, to take part as it were, in the workings of the ancestral mind. He, in turn, again by means of language, perpetuates and enriches the thoughts, feelings, and prejudices of past generations for the benefit of posterity. In this way language embodies the living manifestation of historical continuity and the psychological matrix in which man's awareness of his distinctive social heritage is aroused and deepened.[27]

In Herder's view, tradition fueled the "continuous spiritual genesis" of culture. But underlying all his speculations was something very much like philosophical anarchism, in which the integrity of each individual represents the highest social value. Like later philosophical anarchists, Herder felt that ultimately each group would establish its own needs without the requirements of formal social organizations and, clearly, without a central authority.

Herder was a Lutheran cleric, and he may have equated the idea of *Humanität* with the millennium. This international stage might have seemed to him only a remote goal, seen like a distant star. But the idea of it, or of aspiring to it, attracted many American thinkers in the early nineteenth century, who could see the relevance of Herder's ideas to their society. Everything in his work stressed a conception of pluralism, the awareness of individual integrity, and the need for egalitarianism. His interest in folk song and folklore was based on a radical conception of cultural relativism, which as Isaiah Berlin has noted proclaims the "equal validity of incommensurable cultures."[28] Americans interested in his work (among them Emerson, Whitman, and Constance Rourke) read him with great accuracy and understood the relevance of his positions for developments in the United States.

The United States lacked a peasantry comparable to that of Herder's Germany, but the great variety of separate groups (often in non-agrarian vocations) who populated the country from the first has made the central implications of folk the same for us as it was for Herder. In Herder's Germany, creativity was most manifest in the peasantry, but he understood that it did not arise from a special talent or a particular class. Rather, it was ordinary—an attribute of all humanity—and was most vividly displayed in the folk arts of those least dependent on "official culture."

In the United States, Herder's ideas prefigured what in recent times has been called the "roots phenomenon," a phrase that derives from both the book and the enormously popular television series based on the work of Alex Haley.[29] Haley's attempts to discover the roots of his family in Africa seemed to strike a chord in the hearts not only of African Americans but of all ethnic Americans. The widespread interest *Roots* generated speaks directly to Herder's assertion that all people need to associate themselves in a positive way with their cultural antecedents, and this is especially true in a nation like ours where a sense of the past is often denied and minorities are often persecuted simply because they are different from the majority. Herder recognized that although the idea of individual freedom is crucial, human beings have an equally strong need to function in close association with their compatriots and to celebrate a common history. As Haley's book explained, African Americans could not find an equal place in American society without first acknowledging their folk antecedents. Only then would it be possible to hope for a full and integrated status among all other groups.[30]

What is most remarkable is that Herder's followers in Germany generally distorted his ideas. Several generations of German folklorists misconstrued the broadly humane concerns that permeated Herder's philosophy and posited in their place a spurious connection between folklore, nationalism, and racism. And because of the horrifying results of German chauvinism in the twentieth century, modern scholars have often been tempted to read back into Herder's views some similar implications.

I first encountered Johann Gottfried Herder in my reading of Emerson and Whitman[31] but since came to realize that many teachers of folklore attribute to him the idea of "Romantic Nationalism," a catch phrase that means racism and chauvinism. I have never encountered a recent dissertation in folklore that does not routinely repeat this calumny.[32] Folklorist Albert B. Friedman's brief discussion of Herder typifies the continuing and often subtle attribution to Herder of racist ideas: "A race could not fulfill itself or carry out its sacred duty so long as its unique spirit was contaminated. The *Volkslied* [Herder coined the term in 1771] was, thus, one of several touchstones by which the community could measure its approach to, or declension from, purity."[33]

But, in fact, nothing could be further from racist ideology than Herder's philosophy, and indeed the philosophical anarchism of his thought forced him to play down its egalitarian implications. Emerson, Whitman, and other American Herderians, addressing the needs of a new democratic culture, were not so constrained.

# THREE

## Herder and American Folk Tradition

True to the ideas of the Romantic era that he helped to bring into existence, Herder tried to replace a mechanistic philosophy with an organic approach that underscored the interaction of body and soul, matter and mind, and ultimately individual and society. His ideas had an astonishing and quite unforeseen impact in the United States of the early nineteenth century, a society then seeking quite consciously to define itself. In a Germany still bound to the caste system of feudalism, the whole network of Herder's thought threatened to expose its radicalism at every point. He therefore played down its egalitarian aspects, features that are still not always obvious to modern readers living, as Robert T. Clark, Jr., put it, "on this side of the French Revolution and the Romantic Movement.[1]

American writers in the nineteenth and twentieth centuries unveiled the democratic affirmations in Herder's philosophy. But their ideas of democracy rested not on local or regional developments but on the idea of universal natural rights, largely derived from the theories of John Locke.

Lockean theory was based on an imaginary anthropology rather than on empirical evidence. It simply asserted a "state of nature" in which all people had certain basic rights, among them life, liberty, and property; in America, the last term was changed to accommodate a populace largely devoid of property. The acceptance of Locke's ideas exemplifies an irony of the modern world: as Alfred North Whitehead has observed, the new philosophy's goal was rationalism, but at crucial points in the arguments of such writers as Isaac Newton and Locke, it became necessary to rely on simple affirmations of faith.[2] As Newton had to assume the existence of hard, concrete elements that could be called matter, so Locke assumed the existence of natural rights without historical evidence.

Herder's position, however, was both anti-Enlightenment and anti-Lockean, and it consequently moved in an entirely different direction. Herder provided a major and unique justification for democratic ideology based on a concrete demonstration of the creative powers of the lower classes. Unlike the Enlightenment argument assuming universal laws of equality, Herder's work showed how the creations of the peasantry are the stuff of which national literatures are made; indeed, he argued, folk song and folk speech have a beauty and efficacy in their own right that formally trained poets can never imitate successfully. Jefferson had argued that a democracy was the best form of government because it would allow the occasional "diamond in the rough" to make a contribution to the society. Herder identified the diamond mine itself.

The democratic inferences to be drawn from Herder's views are not simply incidental to his work as a whole. Although overlooked by his immediate followers, there is, as Berlin has noted, a conception of individualism in Herder that is "closer to the anarchism of Thoreau or Proudhon or Kropotkin . . . than to the [authoritarian] ideals of Fichte or Hegel or political socialists. . . . He stands with those who protest against mechanization and vulgarization rather than with the nationalists of the last hundred years, whether moderate or violent."[3] Berlin finds Herder's notion of "the equal validity of incommensurable cultures" even more threatening to the conventional attitudes of Western thought than the skepticism of Hume. So radical a principle that makes it impossible to judge any culture by the standards of another, also anticipates the arguments of anthropologists like Claude Lévi-Strauss who, as we have seen, refuse to make any qualitative distinctions between the "savage mind" (that is, mythic thought) and contemporary thought processes. One can easily imagine how unsettling so profound a critique of accepted caste and class attitudes would have been had Herder given them full play. He was forced to omit from his work some of his strongest observations. He insisted that "only one class exists in a state, the *people* (not the mob), and to it belong king and peasant, each in his place, in the sphere determined for him." In response to an opposite view Kant expressed, he wrote, "The man who needs a master is an animal; as soon as he becomes human, he no longer needs any master at all."[4] In a comment that appeared in his notebook, Herder affirmed that "political reform has to come from below."[5] But the public was not aware of these dimensions of Herder's work until they were published as part of the scholarly apparatus of the Suphan edition, the fourteenth volume of which (containing the last two parts of the *Ideen*) appeared in 1909. From 1791 to 1909, the world knew only a selective version of Herder's ideas. As Clark points out, "Like his most important predecessor, Leibnitz, he was forced to retain his best philosophy for himself."[6] Berlin maintains that "Herder's most characteristic descendants were to be found in Russia. . . . In that country his ideas entered the thought of those critics and creative artists who not merely developed national and pseudo-national forms of their own native art but became passionate champions of all 'natural,' 'spontaneous,' traditional forms of art and self-expression wherever they manifested themselves. These admirers of ethnic color and variety . . . so far from supporting authority and repression, stood politically on the left, and felt sympathy for all forms of cultural self-expression, especially on the part of the persecuted minorities—Georgians, Poles, Jews, Finns, and also Spaniards, Hungarians, and other 'un-reconstructed' nations. . . . All this is typically Herderian."[7]

This is not a totally misleading comment, although the European Herderians tended, as Berlin suggests, to be interested in "color" rather than in more deeply rooted implementations of Herder's theories. And it is hard not to recall Herder when we consider the amazing resurgence of freedom movements among the Eastern European states only recently liberated from Stalinist colonialism.

But like most of Herder's modern critics, Berlin misses the most complete and far reaching influence of Herder's ideas, which took place in the United States, beginning in the nineteenth century and continuing to the present time. The heritage of Herderian thought as it was understood in the nineteenth-century United States was extremely close to the spirit of his authentic views. It was here that it achieved its most complete and far-reaching influence, in part because of the general theoretical commitment to democratic and egalitarian ideology in the United States. Many of Herder's formulations have had persistent meaning within the specific conditions of American experience—the emphasis on folklore as the foundation for national culture; the effort to provide legitimacy for American English (and vernacular diction) as well as for the reaction against the cultural subservience to Europe (and especially Britain); the use of folk ideology as a means of balancing collective responsibility with a fundamentally individualistic and anarchistic tendency in society; and finally, the creation of a developed and sophisticated society that will eternally keep itself open to the salutary influence of folk tradition. In one of his rare comments on Britain's American colonies, Herder wrote: "Perhaps when the arts and sciences shall become decadent in Europe, they will arise there with new blossoms, with new fruit." But even Herder would have been surprised to know what fertile soil his conceptions would find in this country.

Herder's ideas were known in America from the first decade of the nineteenth century. As early as 1824 Emerson's brother William had written from Germany, "Read all of Herder you can get." And in 1829 Emerson borrowed from the Harvard College library Churchill's 1803 translation of the *Ideen*. The American historian George Bancroft wrote an essay on Herder's thought for the influential *North American Review* in 1825. (Bancroft had done all his graduate study in Germany, receiving his Ph.D. in 1820.) And two years after James Marsh's translation of *The Spirit of Hebrew Poetry* (still the only translation of the work in English) appeared in 1833, the American Transcendentalist George Ripley wrote a fifty-six-page "Life of Herder" for *The Christian Examiner*. Herder's exegesis of biblical texts had particular meaning to the American religious educator Calvin E. Stowe, who wrote in 1829:

> If you would ascertain the great principles on which you must judge of the Hebrew poetry, and become acquainted with its characteristic features, study [Robert] Lowth; if you desire to know more of the precise idea which the Hebrew poets intend to express, and to trace with philological accuracy the sources of their language and imagery, follow the criticism of [Johann David] Michaelis; but if you

would lay aside the philosopher and critic and give yourself up to intellectual enjoyment, if you would have the same sensations and the same thoughts, while chanting the Hebrew poetry, which the Hebrews themselves had, catch the tuneful notes of Herder.[8]

Churchill's and Marsh's translations seemed to speak most directly to New England Transcendentalists and theologians. For his part, Emerson was attracted to Herder's ideas in manifold ways. He was impressed by Herder's organic theory of the relationship between humankind and nature and the humanistic theology that developed from it. Herder himself was not drawn to mystical religion and was not a "transcendentalist" in any sense, but he was nevertheless a forerunner of the Romantic tradition that Emerson and his Transcendentalist compatriots inherited from Europe. Herder's concern with the question of nationalism, however, could not fail to interest Emerson during this period, which literary historians now refer to as the "American Renaissance." In fact, there were many startling similarities (and some important differences) between Herder's Germany and the United States in the early decades of the nineteenth century.

In both societies, writers were judged on how closely their work resembled prestigious models from abroad, and anyone who dared to diverge from the conventional styles was ridiculed. Emerson and other proponents of American cultural sovereignty found their culture in almost total dependence on the values of European critics. The same was true in the terms of language itself; a writer who attempted to employ a level of diction that varied from British English was attacked for using "barbaric" American English. (Whitman's "barbaric yawp" was a conscious response.) Like Herder before him, Emerson had to frame his program for literary independence within the context of a demand that American English be accepted as the language of the nation's literature. It was Emerson who first attempted to establish a relationship between folk and formally organized literary traditions for the purpose of defining the essential character of this country. As early as 1826 he had written in his *Journals,* "Ballads, bon mots, anecdotes give us better insights into the depths of past centuries than grave and voluminous chronicles," and in *Nature* (1836) he emphasized the germinal power of folk speech. "Because of this radical correspondence between visible things and human thoughts, savages, who have only what is necessary, converse in figures," Emerson wrote in the chapter "Language." "As we go back in history, language becomes more picturesque, until its infancy, when it is all poetry; or all spiritual facts are represented by natural symbols. . . . It has moreover been observed that the idioms of all languages approach each other in passages of the greatest eloquence and power. And as this is the first language, so is it the last."[9] The influence of Herder is unmistakeable. Emerson realized that creativity does not arise from earlier traditions; it is always available directly to human culture. For Emerson, as for Herder, imitation of any kind was cultural suicide.

Unlike Herder's European followers, Emerson drew a major corollary from the folk ideology. In his view, folk tradition is not only the basis on which the national culture is constructed; it can also be the means by which the developed literary tradition may be revived when it begins to lose its original power—hence, it is the first and last source of creative power. Thus for Emerson, folk traditions had political as well as esthetic dimensions:

> The corruption of man is followed by the corruption of language. When the simplicity of character and the sovereignty of ideas is broken up by the prevalence of secondary desires—the desire of riches, of pleasure, of power, and of praise—and duplicity and falsehood take the place of simplicity and truth, the power over nature as an interpreter of the will is lost; new imagery ceases to be created, and the old words are perverted to stand for things which are not; a paper currency is employed, when there is no bullion in the vaults. In due time, the fraud is manifest and words lose all power to stimulate the understanding or the affections.[10]

The antidote to such stagnation, Emerson believed, was to return to the folk sources of the culture.

Unlike Herder, American writers could take full account of the democratic affirmations of his theory. In *A Backward Glance O'er Travel'd Roads,* Whitman pointed out, "two items for the imaginative genius of the West, when it worthily rises—First, what Herder taught to the young Goethe, that really great poetry is always (like the Homeric or Biblical canticles) the result of a national spirit, and not the privilege of a polish'd and select few; Second, that the strongest and sweetest songs yet remain to be sung."[11] Whitman took even more literally than Emerson Herder's proposal that a national literature should be based on the creations of the folk. Grafting this point of view onto his own fiercely democratic ideology, he constructed a unique adaptation of Herder's position on the people's creative power to the conditions of American society. Herder had argued that recognizing the value inherent in folk art might bring into existence a humanistic, democratic culture. Whitman began with the assumption of political democracy and then, like Emerson, emphasized the irony of America's dependence on the aristocratic literary culture of Europe.

To Whitman as to Herder, the artist's discovery and development of folk speech was the key to cleansing and revitalizing literature. Whitman realized that language is not the creation of pedants but is an ongoing process that comes from the decisions of the people. And just as Homer and the biblical bards had created their poetry out of the language of the folk, so modern bards must find their inspiration and materials in the language and diction of the common people of their own culture. Whitman's concept of slang embodies these ideas:

> [slang is] the lawless germinal element, below all words and sentences, and behind all poetry, and proves a certain perennial rankness and protestantism in speech. As the United States inherit by far their most precious possession—the language they talk and write—from the Old World, under and out of its feudal institutes, I will allow myself to borrow a simile even of those forms farthest removed from American democracy. Considering Language then as some mighty potentate, into the majestic audience-hall of the monarch ever enters a personage like one of Shakespeare's clowns, and takes position there, and plays a part even in the stateliest ceremonies. Such is slang or indirection, an attempt of common humanity to escape from bald literalism, and express itself illimitably, which in pre-historic times gave the start to, and perfected, the whole immense tangle of the old mythology.[12]

Unlike contemporary folklore scholars, Whitman saw in slang obvious sources of a subversive tradition that consciously undermines the values of the establishment. Slang subverts conventional literature as religious dissenters (the protestants) subverted the established church and as the court jester punctures the pomposity of monarchy. (In Shakespeare, of course, the fool represents folk wisdom.) Whitman's bold insight is one Herder could never have expressed overtly in his own time.

Although the folklorists and philologists Whitman had been reading tended to limit their analyses of the poetry-making abilities of the folk to primitive societies, Whitman claimed to have discovered the same mechanisms at work in the cities of the United States. "I find the same rule in the people's conversations everywhere," he wrote. "I heard this among the men of the city horsecars, where the conductor is often call'd a 'snatcher.' . . . In the slang of New York common restaurant waiters a plate of ham and beans is known as 'stars and stripes,' codfish balls as 'sleeve buttons,' and hash as 'mystery.' "[13] Whitman was describing what folklorists came to call "the folk process," a still imperfectly understood method whereby the folk fashion the figurative elements of language and a process Herder was among the first to define.

Whitman's perspicacity helps to explain why, except for a few early pieces, he wrote no literary ballads. He boasted of his emancipation from what he called the "ballad style" of poetry, a form dependent on a meter and rhyme borrowed from dramatic-narrative folk songs. For the English and German Romantic poets as well as most nineteenth-century American writers, imitation of traditional ballads seemed the most appropriate way to use folk tradition. (Goethe, after all, had written literary ballads in response to what he mistakenly thought was Herder's program.) Whitman was unique in his resistance to the mere copying of forms derived from ballads that, as he noted, were based on legends about royalty and aristocracy and were thus not fit for the poet of democracy. Critics have often commented on the lack of folk influences in Whitman's poetry. But it is more accurate to say that Whitman rejected superficial expressions of folklore—such as, for example, Longfellow's *Song of Hiawatha*—in favor of a more thoroughgoing program based on the real teachings of Herder, of reinventing himself. In such a poem as "Song of Myself," perhaps the best long poem in American tradition, Whitman appears to be creating a national expression akin to epic. But in fact, he rejected the conventional form in favor of a new style he called "free verse."

Like Emerson, Whitman knew that it is the poet who inherits the language of his people. Long before Yeats and Eliot, he knew it was his responsibility to "purify the language of the tribe," raising it on his own terms to its highest possible level. Without Herder, the efforts Emerson and Whitman made to promote and describe a native culture may not have been as fruitful. And largely because of his influence, the works of Emerson and Whitman became an extremely fertile resource for later artists and folklorists interested in the same sort of discovery. Joseph J. Kwiat has noted that Emerson's ideas gave foundation to the painter Robert Henri's "already critical attitude toward the smug, hypocritical, provincial cultural state of his native country." While Emerson's work inspired Henri to work through his art to free American culture "from the enervating grasp of the Academy and the Genteel Tradition," Whitman was even more meaningful: to Henri, he was a "force for freedom."[14]

Herder's ideas were applied even more consciously to the conditions of American life by Constance Rourke, whose accomplishments in the field of folk arts are increasingly appreciated. In her major work, *American Humor: A Study of the National Character,* Rourke's first objective was to offset the assertion by many of her contemporaries that American civilization had little to offer in the arts.[15] The history of this assumption is long and complicated, but Rourke responded to one of its most persistent formulations—that the United States was brought into existence under circumstances that denied it the gestation time necessary for a mature and textured culture to develop. What this view really meant to assert was, Rourke argued, exactly what Herder had maintained—that no nation can create a formal, fine art tradition unless it has a folk culture to build it upon. If there is a distinctive literary tradition in this country, she argued, there must be a matrix of folk (and even popular) materials behind it. Later, in *The Roots of American Culture and Other Essays,* Rourke argued that a nation's literature is legitimately its own when it arises from the folklore of its people, a view she specifically identified with Herder.[16]

Rourke acknowledged that, having been denied a feudal era, or what might be called a period of folk accumulation, the United States could easily be seen as a derivative and inferior culture. The idea, she wrote, "was inevitably accepted in the colonial era and has been further defined, elaborated and added to explicitly or otherwise until it stands as a main approach to the study of our culture and even our political, social and economic history."[17] In an effort to show the relevance of Herder's ideas to an understanding of the sources and the significance of American culture, Rourke took pains to point out how they had been misconstrued:

> A mild nostalgia quickly took the place of Herder's bold concept of the folk as a living wellspring of poetry and song. This was brought about mainly through the selective work of Schlegel and the Grimms, whose explorations of folklore and folk-song had great value but who developed to an extreme the romantic concept of primitive or folk-life which had first been touched upon by Montaigne. Antiquarianism began to cast its long insidious spell, and inquiries as to the folk-arts came to be regarded as minor excursions into the pretty or quaint."[18]

Rourke apprehended Herder's great insight that, far from being incidental, the folk roots of a culture were the basis for its continuing development among the nations of the world. In the Foreword to *American Humor,* she declared that the existence of an "American character" was indisputable, a fact she wished neither to defend nor dispute. Her study had instead "grown from an enjoyment of American vagaries, and from the belief that these have woven together a tradition which is various, subtle, sinewy, scant at times but not poor."[19] The United States, she argued, had deep and proliferating folk roots; American folk tradition suffered not from a paucity but an embarrassment of riches.

The work of John and Alan Lomax, the folklorists most responsible for identifying the nature of a specifically American folk song tradition, was also permeated by Herderian values. In *Folk Song: U. S. A.* (1947), the final collaboration of this pioneering father-and-son team, Alan Lomax asserted that "when the American folksinger is understood, when you come to know him, you will be prepared to meet his kinfolk in Russia, China, Spain, Ireland, or wherever oral song lives, for in songs and folklore one encounters ancient bonds that link the races and the nations into the big family of humanity."[20] In their attitudes toward nationalism, their democratic affirmation of folk song, their sense of the certain persistence of folk art within modern societies, and their elevation of national culture to the level of internationalism—in all these, the Lomaxes codified the main conceptions of Herder and the way his ideas have continued to play a part in modern intellectual history.[21]

In order to apply Herder's folk ideology to American circumstances, the differences between this society and the one in which he formulated his philosophy need to be taken into account. When Herder talked about *German* folklore, he assumed that there was a clear and easily identified monolithic treasury of folk tradition. In fact, as was also the case in many European countries at the time, there were a number of folk sources besides those that could be called German. But given the need of the time for political unity in Germany and the drive for political freedom, it seemed essential to choose one central and widespread source to represent the German nation. Herder paid only slight attention to other materials that existed.

Much as Herder had narrowed his view of the German folk, early collectors and folklorists in the United States determined that their main task was to collect American versions of the ballads that had been brought here from the British Isles.[22] But in the United States, multicultural tradition was never far from sight, and Western liberal tradition encompasses a much larger notion of freedom. The Lomaxes were among the first to emphasize that American folk tradition could not be comprehended without taking into account the tremendously widespread interaction between African sources (which quickly became African-American) and the legacy of Anglo-Celtic culture. Hispanic and Latino folk sources were also notable from early times in many sections of the country, especially in the Southwest and West. And within the small compass of our national existence, many other ethnic sources were implanted and only waiting for the proper moment to blossom. For those like Whitman who declared even before the major periods of immigration that the United States was a "teeming nation of nations," the genius of American culture was not in its purity but in its rapid absorption of many different traditions.

Just as Herder's European model should have acknowledged more than one folk source for what ultimately became the German nation (in France as well, there was a strong Celtic component which was not recognized until recently), a more accurate approximation of folk sources in the United States should include not only the Anglo-Celtic but also, among others, Native American, African-American, Hispanic, Latino, Mexican-American, Asian-American,

Puerto Rican, French, Cajun, Creole, German-American, Polish-American, Scandinavian, Italian, Jewish—all representing an unlimited number of possible syncretic configurations.[23] On this Whitmanesque catalogue rests the basis for identifying our society in multicultural terms and setting to rest persistent claims that the United States is an "Anglo-Saxon country."

Moreover, our ethnic sources have to be understood differently from those of most other societies. Many countries contain "minority" cultures whose traditions are encouraged and supported by the government, which usually is controlled by a majority group—in China, the Han; in the former Soviet Union, the Russians. One can still see in those countries the clear differences among the various groups whose folk traditions diverge sharply from each other. But these various styles remain independent and show little influence on each other. In the United States, however, there is no single, dominant folk style from which many independent streams branch off. The functional element in this country is a syncretism that takes elements from many traditions and creates a great number of related but distinct styles. There is, in fact, an underlying and unifying force in American folklife, and it does not emerge from the dominant culture. Its source is the African-American minority tradition, which by all prophecy was expected to disappear. The unifying force is African American and that is as startling a development as if one were to argue, for example, that all of Chinese culture should be directed not by its Han origin but from a subject and outlying province with no political or economic power whatsoever, say, in Inner Mongolia. Yet that is precisely what occurred (and still occurs) in American culture.

Despite the many diverse traditions that need to be taken into account, the determining factors in American culture, especially in the realm of music, come from an admixture with black sources—whether the original tradition was Anglo-Celtic, French, German, Hispanic, Latino, Jewish, or Italian. In 1947, Alan Lomax was the first to point this derivation out:

> The amazing popularity of "John Henry," "Frankie," and other Negro ballads among white singers, the tremendous enthusiasm of all Americans, no matter what their prejudices, for Negro folk music, and the profound influence of this music on American culture—all

this denies the effect of Jim Crow at this level of human communication. From the beginning, Negroes and whites have swapped tunes, tales, dances, and religious ideas. And in the even more basic areas of speech and motor behavior this meeting of minds between the two groups is clearer still. White Americans, perhaps attracted by the exotic rhythms and earthy poesy of Negro song, have been deeply stirred by the poignant sorrow, the biting irony, and the noble yearning for a better world implicit there. And with every passing year American music becomes more definitely an Anglo-African blend. In American folk song, indeed—*A man ain't nothin' but a man.*[24]

Despite the fact that the United States remains one of the most racially segregated societies, it is without doubt the most integrated musically. And while Lomax was describing mainly a syncretism involving Anglo-Celtic and African-American sources, similar exchanges were taking place among a whole range of ethnic sources as well. African-American styles became the underlying power of Hispanic, French (Cajun and Zydeco), and many other American cultural groups.[25]

More than any other field, American music symbolizes the general development of American culture and its reliance on the vast resources of its ethnic inheritance. The irrational racism and ethnic hatreds in our society are revealed as even more inexplicable and outrageous in view of the manifold intercultural relationships that are equally obvious to the eye. It justifies the joke I always use when abroad to explain the differences between American and other strategies of humor. A person goes into a Chinese restaurant for a meal. When the waiter arrives, he turns out to be black. The customer is taken aback but decides to try to be cool. "What's the specialty of the house?" she asks.

With no hesitation the waiter responds, "Pizza."

"Now that does it," the customer exclaims. "This is a Chinese restaurant, the waiter is black, and the specialty of the house is pizza! How come?"

"You must understand," the waiter replies; "this is a Jewish neighborhood."[26]

In the United States, we accept and understand the incongruity of such humor because it mirrors the deep though often confused nature of our ethnic interactions. And although music is the best paradigm of these deep-rooted traditions, there are comparable circumstances in our literary traditions that only now are coming into clear focus.[27] As early as 1922, when he was writing for his college newspaper, William Faulkner offered the view that "a national literature can not spring from folk lore—though heaven knows, such a forcing has been tried often enough—for America is too big and there are too many folklores: Southern negroes, Spanish and French strains, the old west, for these will always remain colloquial; nor will it come through our slang, which is likewise indigenous to restricted portions of the country."[28] Faulkner was quite accurate in his insight but wrong, I believe, in the inferences he drew from it. Cordelia Candelaria has attempted by contrast to "apprehend the full reality of the ethnoracial experience *in* and *of* America":

> [I]n the last two decades many scholars in the arts and humanities have finally begun to recognize that the Eurocentric canon of knowledge originates from and reflects a right-wing protectionist ideology. Using the notion of "universalism" as its *raison d'etat,* this right-wing ideology actively works at protecting the exclusionary tradition that valorizes the culture of patriarchy and its hierarchy of White male privilege. . . . Seen inclusively, the literary production of the Americas includes writings and oral language art forms in Nahuatl, Navajo, Iroquois, Spanish, French, Portuguese, Creole, and numerous other languages including English. . . . Even within the United States, with its vast hybrid of native and immigrant cultures, multilingualism and biliteracy are more consistent with the country's actual pluralism than the English language monolingualism espoused for U.S. public education by the influential right-wing special interest groups protecting the status quo."

And Candelaria notes that it is also true though rarely acknowledged "that U.S. ethnic art and literature are *not* recent post–1960s phenomena resulting from the counterculture movements of that decade. Rather, they date back to the pre-American past of Native myth and legend, to the belles lettres of the Spanish Colonial period, to the mestizo balladry of New Spain, to the antebellum African American narratives and song. . . . The *roots* of ethnic identified U.S. American literature are thus ancient in both 'Old' and 'New' World terms. The *genesis* of that literature dates as far back as the sixteenth-century European conquests, and it was followed by a development seasoned by centuries of American history and custom."[29] Thus, in fact, America had a period of primitive accumulation, the very lineage critics have declared to be lacking in the American experience. At the same time, these comments are very much in line with a general re-evaluation of attitudes toward the nature of culture in the United States, veering consciously from the idea, as expressed by Leo Marx, a leading American studies specialist, that we need "to demonstrate the extent to which American society, for good or evil, is chiefly to be understood as a development of Anglo-European history."[30]

If these movements remind us of Herder's formulations, there is an additional element in musical developments which recalls his prediction that the stage following nationalism will be an internationalism joining together the various strands emanating from the voices of the folk. Perhaps the most obvious indication of Herder's relevance to an understanding of American culture is the persistent echo of "world beat" music in the 1980s, most notably Paul Simon's million-selling album, *Graceland*. Despite its controversial rewriting of South African songs, Simon's production made highly visible a trend to absorb African folk-pop styles into American music. Jon Pareles analyzed this music in the *New York Times*:

> [It] lilts along with harmonies that are always consonant, and it revolves around the three major chords—and, usually, the ¾ beat and four-bar phrases—that are also basic to rock-and-roll. British, East Indian, European, North African and American music have all had a continuing impact on South African pop . . . Zulu choruses, for instance, made connections with hymn-singing (via British missionaries), jubilee songs (from black American minstrels) and more modern gospel and soul music, while retaining vocal interjections and a rhythmic sophistication that are unmistakably African. Ladysmith Black Mambazo, the a cappella Zulu-Swazi chorus that recorded with Mr. Simon and that has three albums available in the United States, won't sound alien to anyone who's heard the Five Blind Boys, the Four Tops or the Persuasions.[31]

Like reggae, an African-Jamaican music that incorporates and revives many American traditions, South African materials can be easily received because Americans have already become accus-

tomed to the basic elements of African styles, including highly syncopated rhythms, call-and-response techniques, and the dance approaches essential to all African music.

National Public Radio music producer Tom Schnabel has observed that "unlike the recordings made by ethnomusicologists
who wandered around rural villages, microphones in hand, [World
Beat originates] in recording studios, often in London and Paris,
reflecting the cities' growing multi-ethnic populations. World Music
has several important subtexts, too: It is about the planet's getting
smaller, the rise of global communications and the introduction of
technology to Third World cultures." As proof of this assertion,
Schnabel reported that a major World Music company introduced
Israeli superstar Ofra Haza, whose rendition of a Yemenite prayer
topped the German pop lists for nine weeks.[32]

The greatest resistance to Herder and the influence of his ideas
comes from those who are concerned about the implications of
relativism. It has been possible to attack the idea of equality on the
ground that, empirically, human beings are not at all equal in most
respects. And if the assumptions on which Lockean egalitarianism
rests turn out to be a matter of faith, then the entire construct is
jeopardized. In the absence of any concrete evidence of absolute
equality it seems absurd to attribute creative or expressive powers
to the lowest echelons of society, and sometimes fierce defenders
of democracy become disillusioned with their advocacy and find
themselves in an elitist or even completely anti-democratic frame
of mind. Such predicaments have been the subject matter of much
contemporary literature and philosophy and have motivated a
shift among some thinkers from glorification of the folk to an acceptance of the tyrannical role of the "superman" (a concept Herder
explicitly rejected). But as Arthur M. Schlesinger, Jr., has observed,
nationalism may be provincial and mean-spirited rather than cos-
mopolitan in its broad aims and heroic in its action.[33]

> Take a look at the world around us today. Most of the organized killing
> now going on is the consequence of absolutism: Protestants and
> Catholics killing each other in Ireland; Muslims and Jews killing each
> other in the Middle East; Sunnites and Shiites killing each other in the
> Persian Gulf; Buddhists and Hindus killing each other in Ceylon;

Hindus and Sikhs killing each other in India; Christians and Muslims killing each other in Armenia and Azerbaijian; Buddhists and Communists killing each other in Tibet. "We have," as Swift said, "just enough religion to make us hate, but not enough to make us love."[34]

Commenting on the absolutist tendencies of Allan Bloom's, *The Closing of the American Mind,* Schlesinger has argued that the American mind is in fact "by nature and tradition skeptical, irreverent, pluralistic and relativistic." And he has implicitly explained the great attraction of Herder to seminal thinkers in the United States: "Absolutism is abstract, monistic, deductive, ahistorical, solemn, and it is intimately bound up with deference to authority. Relativism is concrete, pluralistic, inductive, historical, skeptical and intimately bound up with deference to experience. Absolutism teaches by rote; relativism by experiment. 'I respect faith,' that forgotten wit Wilson Miezner once said, 'but doubt is what gets you an education.' "[35]

Folklorists have tended to lose confidence in the creative power of ordinary people even when they pay lip service to the idea that *folk* refers to lower class and often alienated people. In his wide-ranging study of the Girard collection at the Museum of International Folk Art, Henry Glassie discusses the work of many folk artists. But he confesses that "the nationalistic definition of folklore featured the common people on the assumption that the poorer rural people held the native culture most completely, while the wealthier urbanites were off whoring after foreign fashion. That might have been true in eighteenth-century England or nineteenth-century Hungary, and it may be true today in parts of India or Peru. In our world, however, poor people often gain access to alien ideas through the mass media. Justly angry about their estate, they abandon old culture, while wealthier people who have reason to maintain the status quo, and reason to fear the international orientation of the lower orders, become caretakers of tradition."[36] Such approaches recall the persistent views of folklorists that the power of folk tradition is diminished in contemporary societies, especially under the impact of urban and industrial forces. But these notions have little meaning in American culture. American artists from Emerson's time to the present have been able to return to folk traditions precisely because the folk persist within the framework of more formally developed societies. Repeated efforts in this country to revive folk styles serve to reveal the full range of American expression.

Scholars who make no reference to Herder advocate the process he described:

> It seems to me that the way to the cosmopolitan in social terms is through the local, from thence to the national—where heterodoxy is acknowledged as legitimate within the political boundaries of nation-states—and after, to some concretely imaginable cooperation on an international scale leading to the cosmopolitan community, heterodoxy legitimated globally. To be sure, this is to offer a conceptual paradigm—an image, a vision—not a political program; and to imagine the cosmopolitan polyvocal polity in this way is also utopian—but perhaps only in the sense that it does not as yet exist. To imagine it may also be to make a contribution to its existence.[37]

Alas, it needs to be said finally that, like all of us, Herder had feet of clay. Despite many attempts to exonerate Herder from the stigma of anti-Semitism which characterized his culture and his contemporaries, Paul Lawrence Rose provides convincing evidence of numerous anti-Jewish elements in his thought. "To expose what Herder really thought about the Jewish Question," he says, "enables us to judge whether he really was as liberal or humanitarian as his philosophy appears to be at first sight. The Jewish Question is, in fact, a window into his mind, and it suggests that the recent tendency to see his general outlook as liberal and humanitarian is misconceived."[38]

Rose notes that Herder's early views of the Jews as "a patriotic, warlike people, very inventive and noble in religion, a people shaped by the great 'lawgiver Moses' changed when he considered the period following the return from the Babylonian captivity. It was at that point in their history that they became involved in finance, usury, and commerce, the activities that characterized their decline and was the basis for the hatred generated against them throughout the world. Actually, however, Herder insists that 'The people of God,' to whom He Himself had once granted a fatherland, had for millennia, indeed almost from its origin, been a parasitic plant on the stems of other nations; a stock of cunning go-betweens over well-nigh the whole globe, which despite all oppression, nowhere longs for its own honor and dwelling, for a fatherland of its own." In fact, even the great Moses was struggling against what Herder suggests is the true, Jewish national character: "We observe the Jews here only as the parasitic plant that has attached itself to almost all the European nations, and draws more or less on their sap. After the destruction of old Rome, they were yet only few in Europe, but through the persecutions of the Arabs they came in great crowds. . . . During the barbarian centuries they were exchange-men, agents, and imperial servants. . . . They were oppressed cruelly . . . and tyrannously robbed of what they had amassed through avarice and cheating, or through hard work, cleverness, and diligence."[39] Unlike other German critics of the Jews whose vehemence led to demands for their extinction, Herder's sense of the unique quality of every culture led him to admit that "modern Jewry possessed a religious and cultural validity. There was accordingly no need for—in fact, it was undesirable that there should be—a Kantian 'euthanasia of Judaism.'"

Although there are ambiguous comments about the Jews in Herder's work, some of which Rose believes have been mistakenly understood as philosemitic, Herder "held to the essentially illiberal German conviction that the Jews were far too alien and distinct a nation ever to become 'Germans.' All that Herder conceded was that, with proper correction and instruction, they might become enlightened human beings while remaining 'Jews.'" True to his basic thesis, Rose argues that "The German idea of humanity, like the German idea of freedom, must not be misconstrued in Western liberal terms."[40]

It remains only to be said that Herder, despite the liberating elements of his philosophy, is another sad reminder that the virus of anti-Semitism, then as now, seems immune to the influence of the best values of liberal (and as Rose shows) even radical thought. Fortunately, from my point of view, it was the humane elements in his philosophy that were propagated by his American followers.

# FOUR

## Poplore

That most Americans know very little about their nation's folk sources shows in many different ways. When Americans are invited to take part in a sharing of cultures with people from another country, they are often at a loss to know how to contribute. A group of American teachers was invited to sing a folk song at a party in the People's Republic of China where I was a visiting professor. They huddled for a while and then sang a Beatles' tune. One of the problems is that there are actually too many choices in our national songs; they could have sung a cowboy song, an Appalachian ballad, a white or black spiritual, a Spanish, French, Yiddish, or Danish ethnic tune. They seemed confronted not by a bewildering array of choice but by a general unawareness of all their choices.

The complex relationship in the United States between folk and popular culture also accounts in part for this odd but not surprising circumstance. Almost everywhere else in the world (certainly in Europe and Asia) there is a distinct and easily definable relationship between the two. Folk remains largely rural, and its instruments and repertoire express the traditional elements in the society—its inherited folkways and their creative forms. Pop is usually expressed in an urban voice; it rejects most of the inherited elements and leans often toward the materials of other "advanced" and prestigious societies; watered-down versions of classical music are common. Pop components are composed, associated with particular authors, and fluctuate according to commercial market interests and values. More often than not, the songs in popular culture are escapist, deal largely with banal approaches to love (or unrequited love), or represent what are sometimes called novelty pieces—oddball constructions that may emphasize a peculiar approach or lyric. Sometimes ethnic or folk materials make their way into mainline structures through novelty songs, but typically without lasting effect.

In the United States we have had a significantly different history. Almost from the beginning, our popular culture has had a very close and symbiotic relationship with the folk sources of our society. Just as Herder might have predicted, American culture has periodically drawn from its folk sources in order to create a national and truly indigenous culture, continually rejecting borrowed, prestigious foreign sources while moving constantly toward a multicultural approach that fully expresses the diverse nature of American society. At the same time that folk and popular styles continue their own development in both rural and urban regional settings, materials from folk tradition have strongly colored popular expression. Americans consequently hardly recognize their folk sources even though in the popular music of the day they hear reflections of most of the styles that define American folk music. The relationship between the two is so intimate that it makes more sense to talk about poplore rather than folklore in the United States.

Very little of what developed in American folklore took place without the influence of strong popular and commercial sources. Folk means not one uniquely formed tradition but a mixture of many different sources that interacted in complex ways. There is very little disagreement that the strongest elements in this mix came from African sources, which supplied basic rhythmic underpinnings to American music and determined the essential vocal as well as instrumental approaches of all the traditions involved. It is clear, in fact, that the African elements become more and more conspicuous in our musical developments on both the folk and popular levels.[1]

What happened to the heritage of that unique group of emigrants, brought here against their will as slaves, bears closer examination. African-American people are the source of our great national dilemma and symbolize the horrible wrong that the citizens of the United States still cannot expel from their memories or even come to terms with. White observers initially assumed that African culture would be totally assimilated by the dominant culture of the United States. Slaves came from many different regions of Africa (though mainly the western part of the continent), spoke many different languages, and carried the traditions of many different tribes. Once in the United States, they were forcibly prevented from sustaining their native traditions, including language and all cultural activities, especially music and dance. Whites forbade drums because they were often used to send messages that might encourage uprisings. At first, slaves were a small minority and could hardly be expected to maintain their own ideas of culture under the conditions of slavery. Gerald Mullin has estimated that "slaves in Virginia were speaking an adequate amount of English within six months and that they were speaking well in about two and a half years."[2] Among many others, the founders of the American Folklore Society (including influential ballad collectors Francis James Child and George Lyman Kittredge) urged folklorists in 1888 to study black folklore because they were sure that slavery had obliterated nearly all African traditions: "It is proposed to form a society . . . For the collection of the fast-vanishing remains of Folk-Lore in America, namely . . . Lore of Negroes in the Southern States of the Union."[3]

As Melville J. Herskovits was among the first to note, American whites believed that blacks were a people without a past or a culture of their own.[4] Recent research has told quite a different story and has revealed especially both the nature of African acculturation and the extent to which, from early times, African heritage made itself felt on American traditions. The most important and truly eye-opening information is in the outstanding work of Dena J. Epstein, a librarian who has done extensive research on black folk music to the Civil War.[5] Though not an ethnomusicologist, Epstein was sensitive to how little had been done to record the development of music under slavery in the United States and decided to apply library techniques to collect as much antebellum African-American music as she could identify. Epstein's work has made clear how African materials were developed in the United States and how they were integrated from the beginning not only with folk material but with popular traditions as well.

The process began even in the notorious "middle passage." Slaver vessels regularly brought their victims on deck for exercise in order to keep as many of the slaves in saleable condition as possible. As early as 1693, Epstein has noted, the captain of a British ship commented, "We often at sea in the evening would let the slaves come up into the sun to air themselves, and make them jump and dance for an hour or two to our bagpipes, harp, and fiddle, by which exercise to preserve them in health" (8). One mariner who visited a slaver bound for Savannah in 1796 noted, "In the daytime they [slaves] were not allowed to remain in the place where they had slept, but were kept mostly upon the open deck, where they were made to exercise, and encouraged, by the music of their beloved banjar, to dancing and cheerfulness" (10). Epstein's documentation shows clearly also that slaves brought their own instruments with them, largely drums, but also the early versions of what was to become the only characteristic American folk instrument, the banjo.[6]

Epstein has pointed out that although slaves first arrived in the American colonies in 1619, "almost nothing about their music has been found before the end of the seventeenth century, when they were already playing the fiddle" (22). The absence of any record resulted from the premise that black folklife was hardly worth recording and that slave culture would disappear quickly in any case.

But there is no doubt that slaves quickly became proficient in performing on western instruments and were widely known as excellent musicians. Black fiddlers were widely heralded as early as 1694, and newspaper advertisements for runaway slaves often made particular mention of the ability to play well on certain instruments, especially the fiddle. By 1802, Epstein has noted, African-American fiddlers played regularly at the public balls of the New Orleans "Carnaval" (92).[7] Epstein has cited the 1820 death notice in a Richmond newspaper for Sy Gilliat, whom the editors described as "a man of color, very celebrated as a Fiddler, and much caressed by polished society who will long deplore the loss" (116). Like a number of slaves, Gilliat had actually been able to achieve the status of a professional musician even while in slavery. Epstein has also uncovered rare references to women fiddlers such as Clarinda, " 'a pious coloured woman of South Carolina . . . [who]

learned to play on the violin, and usually, on the first day of the week, sallied forth with her instrument, in order to draw persons of both sexes together, who, not having the fear of God before their eyes, delighted like herself, in sinful and pernicious amusement'" (114).

References to the banjo (known by a variety of different names but undoubtedly referring to the same instrument) are widespread both on the mainland and in the West Indies, where many slaves were "broken in" before being sent to the South. As early as 1763, a poem from St. Kitts offered this recommendation:

> On Festal days; or when their work is done;
> Permit thy slaves to lead the choral dance,
> To the wild banshaw's melancholy sound.

An explanatory note on banshaw stated: "This is a sort of rude guitar, invented by the Negroes. It produces a wild pleasing melancholy sound" (32). A glossary compiled by a Loyalist refugee after the American Revolution offered this definition:

*Bandore,* n. A musical instrument . . . in use, chiefly, if not entirely, among people of the lower classes. . . . I well remember, that in Virginia and Maryland the favourite and almost only instrument in use among the slaves there was a *bandore;* or, as they pronounced the word, *banjer.* Its body was a large hollow gourd, with a long handle attached to it, strung with catgut, and played on with the fingers. . . . My memory supplies me with a couplet of one of their songs, which are generally of the improvisatori kind; nor did I use to think the poetry much beneath the music:

> Negro Sambo play fine *banjer,*
> Make his fingers go like handsaw. (34)

Not incidentally, *banjer* remains the current pronunciation by both white and black Southerners.

Epstein's research shows that African traditions were very quickly merged with those that slaves encountered in the New World. And because music and dance are integral to all African tribal activities, it is easy to understand how fully they were acculturated. But while the process is often labeled acculturation, it is more accurate to say that from the very beginning the process was syncretic, involving full intercourse between the African and the host cultures that slaves encountered in the American colonies, especially the Anglo-Celtic folk materials that themselves had already undergone a good deal of change in the New World. As the *Journal of American Folklore* noted in its first issue in 1888, "As respects old ballads . . . the prospects of obtaining much of value is not flattering. In the seventeenth century, the time for the composition of these had almost passed; and they had, in a measure, been superseded by inferior rhymes of literary origin, diffused by means of broadsides and songbooks, or by popular doggerels, which may be called ballads, but possess little poetic interest."[8]

No area of activity could resist the two-way interaction between the slaves' and the masters' culture, a point often missed because the early reactions of whites to slave culture were couched in language of derision and shock. But the evidence actually shows that whites were fascinated and exhilarated, often uncontrollably attracted, to the music and dance of the slaves. "As the eighteenth century progressed," Epstein has observed, "increasing numbers of slaves in the islands and on the mainland learned to play Western instruments and to dance European dances, not necessarily as a substitute for their native recreations, but as a supplement to them. The descriptions of African and European musics and dancing existing side by side demonstrate the process by which acculturation proceeded" (80). She has also pointed out that although there is "no way of knowing, of course, to what degree black fiddlers played African music or added an African coloration to European tunes . . . Negro jigs entered the repertory of white fiddlers and fifers [as] is demonstrated in a number of tutors and collections of pieces" (114). Often white and black musicians traded tunes, as an English traveler reported from Baltimore in 1785: "We sent for a violin in the evening and had a most agreeable dance. . . . After the poor Negro's fingers were tired of fiddling, I took the violin and played them the 'Pleasures of Youth' and the 'Savage Dance' " (115). These and other occasions formed the basis for the close connections between black and white fiddle, banjo, and dance styles—syncretisms that are still too often ignored by American folklorists. The banjo, perhaps the one main exception, is now acknowledged to be a major American folk instrument. Its influence is notable in folk, jazz, Tin Pan Alley popular music, and, more recently, bluegrass music.

That these black influences still too often go unnoticed is plain in the introduction to an influential album of fiddle tunes. "Traditional fiddling in America has its repertorial and stylistic roots in the British Isles of the 18th century," the note maintains. "Irish and Scottish or North Country influences predominate despite the numerical dominance of English settlers."[9] The notes to one of the songs performed by Vermont fiddler Elmer Barton identify a rhythmic pattern that results in syncopation:

> The history of these slurring patterns, which can be said to be the very soul of this widespread fiddling style, is yet to be written, but there is evidence that it is a venerable style with roots in British (probably Irish) fiddling of the late 18th and the early 19th centuries. Syncopation in modern popular music may owe much to this traditional style, which, though usually considered a product of the South, occurs in the performances of traditional musicians such as Elmer Barton with cultural roots far from the South.[10]

As Epstein and other scholars have shown, the influence of black fiddling was widespread, and it is in fact what distinguishes American fiddling styles from British.

The nature of syncretism between black and white traditions can be seen distinctly in two additional major occurrences: the creation of minstrelsy and the development of black spirituals, both of which reveal also the extent of popular and folk coalescence. Critics have always been aware of the important implications of minstrelsy for the movement of African-American materials to white popular audiences, mainly as a means of reinforcing black stereotypes. Many critics agree with Epstein that "minstrel theatre is outside the scope of black folk music, however closely it may have been related" (147). But minstrelsy nonetheless provided the first continuing use by white performers of black materials for a broad, white, popular audience—what music critics call "covering" black music in white styles. As Robert C. Toll has pointed out, "The blend of Afro-and Euro-American musical and dance styles, which later became common in American popular culture, began on the frontier and was first given wide exposure by minstrels."[11] Clearly, too, minstrelsy provided opportunities for materials to pass both ways, which explains how minstrel songs often ended up in the repertoire of black folk musicians. Not only materials but styles as well came together in the characteristic repertoires of both black and white artists.

The most important minstrels were all northerners, but many did "field work" of a sort whose findings they then interpreted for urban audiences. Toll has explained that the minstrel commonly did not act as "the white man in the woodpile" whose songs blacks simply absorbed in their repertoires. Most early minstrels, he has asserted, used Afro-American dances and dance-steps, reproduced individual Negro songs and "routines" intact, absorbed Afro-American syncopated rhythms into their music, and employed characteristically Afro-American folk elements and forms. Black and white Americans influenced each other (50).

In the early period of minstrelsy, northern musicians were often critical of slavery, and their skits showed how slaves cleverly resisted their cruel masters. But Toll has identified a radical shift in the mid-1850s. "The tone of minstrelsy sharply changed as its folk and antislavery content virtually disappeared. . . . They thrust aside wily black tricksters and antislavery protesters for loyal grinning darkies who loved their white folks and were contented and indeed fulfilled by working all day and singing and dancing all night" (88).

As minstrelsy moved further and further from its folk sources, the original blend of African, American, and Anglo-Celtic materials shifted more and more to commercial, popular elements often derived from music hall and other stage sources. While the folk traditions existed alongside their pop and commercial mixtures in rural settings, the main line of American commercial music and theatrical expression was marked forever with African-American music and dance styles. Increasingly, in a variety of fields including literature, these black elements became stronger as American artists reached back to their folk sources for just the reasons Herder had suggested—to rejuvenate national expression. In the early period of minstrelsy, Toll has shown, the minstrels were very aware of the national and democratic values in the new stage traditions they were creating.

As is generally the case with black traditions, we know almost nothing detailed about the nature of the plantation music, one of the main sources of minstrelsy. Hans Nathan has shown that the

white minstrel banjoists have provided us with the only information bearing on plantation instrumental music. The basic instrument of the white minstrels was the five-string banjo, and the music
they played, often filtered through the consciousness of such composers as Dan Emmett and Stephen Foster, reflected the instrumental styles of the black plantation musicians. Because we have no
records of notation for these oral melodies, we will never know
exactly how they sounded. But when, in the 1820s, the minstrels
began to publish banjo method and instruction books to capitalize
on the popularity of the banjo, they included many tunes that were
based on African-American folk styles—which in turn often went
back into both black and white folk traditions. From an analysis
of the tunes contained in these manuals and of the various approaches of black banjo music, whose main characteristic is a complicated syncopation,[12] Nathan has proposed that the roots of jazz
reach much deeper than has commonly been thought:

> Let us for a moment consider the musical activities and interests of
> the antebellum slave of the southern plantation. His African musical
> heritage was discouraged. The folk tunes he heard from his master's
> lips were of Irish and Scottish origin. He sang them himself, no doubt
> with his own words adapted to them. In addition, he played strains
> on his favorite instruments, the banjo and the fiddle. These strains
> are no longer known to us but it is most likely that many of them were
> those of the frontier—namely the folk dance tunes of the British
> Isles. . . . The history of jazz has now been extended backward. It
> does not begin with ragtime, Negro spirituals, or the songs of the
> early popular theater, but with a few dozen banjo tunes which have
> the flavor of the plantation. Although originating about one hundred
> years ago, they furnished the basic elements of an idiom of striking
> contemporaneity. (207, 213)

Nathan may be right about the oldest sources of jazz, but the mix of
elements and the levels of culture involved reveal the merging of
West African and Anglo-Celtic folk and popular styles that had been
occurring since African people first came to this country.[13]

The complexity of minstrelsy has only recently come to light.
"The process by which black people were divested of control over
elements of their culture and generally over their own cultural rep-
resentation, while surely an outcome of the economics of slavery,
was far more complex than studies of minstrelsy have granted," the

historian Eric Lott has argued. "Though blackface was in the business of staging or manufacturing 'race,' that very enterprise was also involved in a *carnivalizing* of race, such that its ideological production became more contradictory, its consumption more indeterminate, its political effects more plural than previously assumed." According to Lott, minstrelsy "produced a popular form in which racial insult was twinned with racial envy, moments of domination with moments of liberation, counterfeit with currency—a pattern at times amounting to no more than the two faces of our particular form of racism, at others gesturing toward a specific kind of political or sexual danger; and all of it comprising a peculiarly American structure of racial feeling."[14]

Lott has argued that white imitators were closer to traditional black performance than has been thought by citing the case of P. T. Barnum. When his blackface minstrel quit, Barnum searched through the dance-houses of New York City until he found and hired a talented African-American break-down dancer. But Barnum quickly discovered that American minstrel audiences uniformly "resented, in a very energetic fashion, the insult of being asked to look at the dancing of a real negro." Barnum's solution was to disguise the black dancer as a minstrel "darky." A black man thus disguised himself as a white man to imitate a black man dancing. He became Barnum's star entertainer. This "counterfeit" of black styles exhibited the underlying power of the genuine tradition, one white audiences deeply admired.

Toll and Nathan have argued that the frontier provided an environment that accelerated the syncretism of black and white folk and popular traditions. Despite continuing criticism of Frederick Jackson Turner's frontier thesis, the example of minstrelsy seems to support Turner's notion that a distinctive American culture arose from the contact between European sources and the American wilderness.[15] The process began with the first European plantations in the East and continued across the continent. Turner maintained that Europeans were conscious of the impact of the wilderness at each point of contact until, by a gradual process of attrition, they were stripped of their Old World characteristics. Turner identified this persistent struggle between East and West as the dynamic of American development, the foundation of a society in which European influences had been eliminated or radically transformed:

> The wilderness, masters the colonist. It finds him a European in dress, industries, tools, modes of travel, and thought. It takes him from the railroad car and puts him in the birch canoe. It strips off the garments of civilization and arrays him in the hunting shirt and moccasin. It puts him in the log cabin of the Cherokee and Iroquois and runs an Indian palisade around him. Before long he has gone to planting Indian corn and plowing with a sharp stick; he shouts the war cry and takes the scalp in orthodox Indian fashion.[16]

Critics have observed that Turner's frontier thesis omitted reference to women and other groups whose role in American culture we are just beginning to recognize. But Turner was clearly aware of the power exercised over European settlers by Native Americans—despite our continuing efforts to disguise their influence.[17] Perhaps his thesis even explains our maniacal attempts to annihilate their cultures. For as Europeans continue to remind us, Americans remain, in their eyes and in many respects, *peaux rouges* (literally, "red skins"). However much Americans have reacted against the identification with Native Americans, such writers as Henry James and Mark Twain have used the relationship as the basis for a characteristic strain of American humor.[18]

The frontier provided the perfect ground for an integration of black and white traditions. Freed from many of the powerful European formal sources of culture and reluctant to accept Native American influence, denizens of the frontier found fertile ground for deep and lasting interaction of the vernacular elements in African-American and Anglo-Celtic traditions. And popular materials had an important role to play in this development.

The minstrel tradition is the first clearly documented historical example of the influence of these elements; Nathan has observed that the earliest minstrel bands, "in spite of strong Negro influence, . . . used various steps of the folk dances of the British Isles. These they had borrowed from the plantation itself, the frontier, and, above all, from theatrical tradition" (95). The career of Dan Emmett illustrates well the interplay of these influences. Born in Ohio, Emmett was one of the most important and prolific minstrel musicians and composers, the author of such tunes as "Dixie."

"Like the oils and water colors of itinerant American painters, Emmett's is a folk art," Nathan has stated. "It speaks only to those who, either out of naïveté or sophistication, are capable of delighting in something that is unpolished and of limited means, but sharply defined and direct" (98). Emmett, like many minstrels, was an "ear musician" who worked without written music. But his approach embodied precisely what I describe as poplore—a commercial, professionally oriented strategy based on a mixture of folk and popular elements. In the Ohio of his youth, Emmett recollected, "it was a fashion in those days among the young people to try their skills at making verses, and sing them to some popular tune" (104). Although he composed some of his own, Emmett continued to use old tunes for his verses. One of his first songs (based on such an old tune) recounted the conflict between a Negro and a Jewish peddlar. Done in African-American dialect, it reveals Emmett's early interest in black minstrelsy. Nathan has pointed out that the use of a Jewish figure in the song "was suggested by English stage music; it does not exist in early American Negro minstrel songs" (110).

Like many minstrels, Emmett learned black styles directly from black performers. But he also learned how to play banjo from two of the best-known white banjo players, one of them Joel Walker Sweeney, who for many years was erroneously identified as the man who added the fifth string to the banjo.[19] With three friends, Emmett formed the first minstrel band, a group that was instantly successful. When he brought its music and comedy to the British Isles in 1843, he introduced the banjo, tambourine, and bones to English and Irish audiences. In this way Emmett played an important role in a series of cultural transactions, beginning with the early influence of British folk styles in the American colonies and concluding with an invasion of the United States by an English band that created an instantaneous sensation here with its Liverpudlian version of rock and roll. Like the Beatles' a century later, Emmett's troupe accelerated the merging of British and American materials. More importantly it introduced additional popular and commercial approaches to the traditional styles of British folk song. The banjo (later in a four-string rather than five-string version), bones, and variations of the tambourine (all marks of the minstrel tradition) became permanently enmeshed in British (especially Irish) musical styles and can be heard there to this day.

The minstrel phenomenon, far from expressing folk art, is in fact poplore—the syncretism of traditional with popular, commercial materials. Minstrelsy arose just prior to the Civil War, an agonizing and crucial moment in American cultural history that ushered in the modern era. From that time on, all artistic expression in America showed the merging of African-American with Anglo-Celtic and other ethnic traditions on a folk as well as a commercial level.[20] On the whole, as Gilbert Chase has explained, "to complete the cycle of borrowings, we should reiterate that many minstrel songs have their origins in anonymous folk tunes, so that they have passed from the domain of folklore and back to it again after the usual process of being modified or 'reworked.' "[21] The results of this process are most notable in our music, but the same constituents were implanted in all levels of American culture. The work of literary humorists and, most notably, of Mark Twain in his masterpiece *Adventures of Huckleberry Finn* (1884) presented for the first time a diction of black and white vernacular expression in widely accessible form.[22]

The creation of the black spiritual also demonstrates the influence of popular sources on folk tradition. Scholars still debate whether white or black sources were the basis for the spiritual's development. But as Gilbert Chase has argued, "That Negro singing in America developed as the result of the blending of several cultural traditions is certain; and it seems equally certain that one of these traditions was the folk style of early New England psalmody and hymnody, carried southward in the late eighteenth and early nineteenth centuries" (239). In notation, Chase has shown clearly how the straightforward melody of "Amazing Grace," one of the best-known religious songs in both black and white tradition, became a highly ornamented folk-like tune among white southern country people. A song of certain authorship but widely accepted in folk tradition,[23] it became even more "relished"[24] when it was absorbed into melismatic, black style.

Chase has also pointed out that the tune "Mississippi," attributed in a popular Southern hymn book to a composer named

Bradshaw, "bears all the earmarks of an eighteenth-century English popular tune" used in a ballad opera and a patriotic song. Similarly, "Long Time Ago," an equally intriguing tune published in William Walker's *Southern Harmony* (1835), was "obviously borrowed from an old Negro song that was already widely known by the time the first edition of *Southern Harmony* appeared in 1835." The history of the song, in Chase's view, is "a striking illustration of the borrowing of materials among different cultural traditions. Although the original Negro version has not been located, we can assume that it existed; thus we have four different traditions represented in the various versions of this song: (1) Negro folk tradition, (2) urban popular tradition (blackface minstrelsy), (3) white rural folk tradition, (4) urban cultivated tradition" (205).

Again, the frontier contributed to this black and white cultural interaction. According to George Pullen Jackson, the African American on the frontier "found himself among real friends—among those who by reason of their ethnic, social and economic background, harbored a minimum of racial prejudice; among those whose religious practice came nearest to what he—by nature a religious person—could understand and participate in."[25] The Lomaxes have made a similar point:

> There is no question about the participation of the Negro in the Great Revival nor should there be about his musical influence upon it. . . . the story of the development of the white spiritual since the early part of the nineteenth century when Negroes were converted in large numbers is one of steady progress toward the most favored Negro song structure—simplicity of language, feeling more important than meaning in the lines, much repetition, choruses coming every four lines, choruses that wander from song to song, refrains coming every line—in essence, the leader-chorus form. There is no doubt that, in the beginning, Negroes took over traditional white spiritual melodies; one can find them by the scores in the early collections of Negro spirituals. But today, you find that the reverse is true; the white revival churches are adopting wholesale melodies and singing styles that have been current among Negroes for some generations.[26]

Characteristically, the old hymns were transformed into camp meeting spirituals by adding choruses to make group singing easier. Chase has shown how the Charles Wesley hymn "He Comes, He Comes, the Judge Severe" was adapted through the addition of the refrain, "Roll, Jordan, roll" (214).[27] Another "dialogue song" (constructed so that men can sing one verse and women the next) is the "Mariner's Hymn," which probably came from a sailor's song resembling the sea chantey "Blow, Boys, Blow" (218).

Chase has identified "a general family resemblance in the basic melodic materials of the three main popular traditions of vocal music that developed in the United States during the first half of the nineteenth century: the revival hymns of the whites, the Negro spirituals and work songs, and the so-called 'plantation' or 'Ethiopian' melodies. What gave to each current or branch its peculiar character," he has stated, "was the 'working over' of the material, the transformation of basic elements through the shaping spirit and the prevailing trend of each tradition, each with its concomitant cultural factors, ranging from ancestral African patterns to vulgarized commercial entertainment" (248). Chase has concluded that the American Negro spiritual attests the "musical syncretism of West African and European elements" (256).

Thus, both secular and religious musical traditions are poplore. Chase has suggested that recently recorded versions of old tunes contain the old tradition "essentially unchanged, because conservatism, in its literal sense of preserving the values of the past, is the essence of folklore" (224). But Chase's analysis illustrates clearly that white and black spirituals were carriers of both musical and social change. They discussed slavery, for example, in ways that were not conservative in any sense. This music embodies a series of stylistic transformations as well as a fundamental rejection of a slave ideology that justified the inferior position of African Americans.

Like other advocates of conservatism among the folk, Richard Dorson missed the significance of this syncretism in black culture. Such transformations of traditional religious behavior are the opposite of conservatism and are the rule rather than the exception in American folklife generally. As Eugene Genovese has pointed out, black religion in America "emptied the content of the slave owners' Christianity while retaining its forms for oppositional or subversive purposes."[28] So rigorous are the formulas of some academics, however, that the contradictions in their systems are as invisible as they are to the balladeers who can sing about a "black, snow-white steed," sticking closely to their formulas despite the real content of the line.[29]

Perhaps the most remarkable (and generally overlooked) example of the nonconservative nature of this process is the influence on black spirituals of a popular (one might say commercial) source—the Bible. Nothing so well illustrates the Herderian folk ideology than the radical transfigurations of biblical imagery by the slave population of the United States. This transformation perfectly exemplified how ordinary human creativity creates an underlying sense of national identity, though unnoticed for the first hundred years of its existence in part because horrific renderings of black dialect obscured the brilliance of the slaves' re-creation of biblical language.[30]

Hundreds of black spirituals illustrate how the locutions of the Bible are transmogrified into the stunning imagery of African-American vernacular language. The process is neither mysterious nor uniquely associated with black tradition; rather it reveals the universal folk genius for working with symbolism, that radical human invention that joins emotional and intellectual expression in language forms that become eternally memorable. As important as any aspect of this development is the black approach to integrating elements from both the Old and the New Testaments, as these migrant verses show:

> God gave Noah the rainbow sign,
> Gonna be the fire not the water next time.
> Sowin' on the mountain, reapin' in the valley,
> You're gonna reap just what you sow.

> If I could, I surely would
> Stand on the rock where Moses stood.

> One of these nights about twelve o'clock,
> This old world's gonna reel and rock.

> Mary wore three links of chain,
> Every link was Jesus name.
> Pharaoh's army got drownded,
> O, Mary, don't you weep.

> He delivered Daniel from the lion's den.
> And Jonah from the belly of the whale,

And the Hebrew children from the fiery furnace,
Then why not every man?

Seek, and you shall find,
Knock, and the door shall be opened,
Ask, and it shall be answered,
And the love comes tumblin' down.

When Israel was in Egypt's land,
Let my people go,
Oppressed so hard she could not stand,
Let my people go.[31]

Black spirituals illustrate the power of the folk in relatively recent times to continue a creative process that in great degree defines the nature of humanity. That so many levels of culture contributed to these seminal cultural materials explains why black culture expresses not only the history and aspirations of African Americans but of all Americans.

Scholars are still attempting to clarify the nature of this cultural relationship. "Settlers from Europe and involuntary settlers from Africa each encountered old cultures from the Old World newly brought by the other group to the New World," Charles Joyner has recently stated. "The only truly old cultures in the New World were Native American cultures. While those may have had more influence on the new transatlantic arrivals than we yet understand, they do not seem to have been nearly so influential as the influence of European and African cultures upon one another. . . . Euro-southerners had their old cultures Africanized by their black neighbors and Afro-southerners had their old cultures Europeanized by their white neighbors."[32] Lawrence W. Levine has argued that "the essence of their [African-American] thought, their world view, their culture, owed much to Africa, but it was not purely African; it was indelibly influenced by the more than two hundred years of contact with whites on American soil, but it was not the product of an abject surrender of all previous cultural standards in favor of embracing those of the white master. This syncretic blend of the old and new, of the African and the Euro-American, resulted in a style which in its totality was uniquely the slaves' own and defined their expressive culture and their world view at the time of emancipa-

tion."[33] Henry Louis Gates, Jr., has noted that the relationship between black and white versions of English illustrates not "a procla-
mation of emancipation from the white person's standard English"
but "the symbiotic relationship between the black and white, between the syntagmatic and paradigmatic axes, between black vernacular discourse and standard English discourse."[34]

Not only the clearly politically oriented spirituals (like "Oh, Freedom," which exclaims, "Before I'll be a slave / I'll be buried in my
grave") but the entire corpus of secular and spiritual black accomplishments testifies to the humanity and genius of even the most
outcast elements of our society. Secular black materials clearly
show the effect of a similar hybridization. Lawrence W. Levine and
others have argued that the secular music of slaves was less impressive than their spirituals because it was "more strictly occasional music: as varied, as narrow, as fleeting as life itself,"[35] but
even if secular and spiritual spheres were less restrictively defined
in slave culture than in our own, it is probably not valid to imply, as
Levine has done, that African Americans are "naturally religious."
Despite many gaps in the record, African-American secular music
in our early history is as exciting and impressive as any spiritual,
especially when we also take into account such major creations
as instrumental (especially banjo and fiddle) styles and dance
traditions.

In our own time, black song has continued to express the highest
spiritual values for the world. The words of such African-American
freedom songs as "We Shall Overcome" reverberate on recordings,
on radio, and on television from South Africa to the People's Republic of China. That song—begun as a church hymn, then adapted for
a tobacco workers' strike, and finally "worked over" by Pete Seeger
as a civil rights anthem—perhaps best exemplifies poplore, the special contribution of the United States to a process that now seems
to be taking place on a global scale.[36] A recent article about South
African Archbishop Desmond Tutu's visit to Los Angeles shortly
after Nelson Mandela was freed from prison suggests as much:

> Sitting in the pulpit of Holman United Methodist Church [in Los An-
> geles] . . . Tutu closed his eyes meditatively, and joined the choir in
> singing "Oh Freedom," an African American spiritual heard often
> during the civil rights movement of the 1960s:

*"And before I'd be a slave*
*I'd be buried in my grave*
*And go home to my Lord and be free."*

Tutu noted the links between the civil rights movement and the liberation struggle in South Africa. "We thank you for the inspiration that we have received from your own civil rights movement. . . . When the missionaries came to our neck of the woods, we had the land and they had the Bible . . . They said, 'Let us pray,' and we foolishly closed our eyes. And when we opened our eyes, we had the Bible and they had the land. . . . The Bible turned out to be an important tool for the oppressed people of South Africa. If you wanted to oppress people, the last thing you should have made available is the Bible because it is the most subversive—the most revolutionary—for those who you would wish to be docile . . . You don't need a Marxist communist manifesto . . . nothing is more radical."[37]

# FIVE

## Folklore, Fakelore, and Poplore

It has always been easier to say what folk is not than to provide a universally acceptable definition of what it is. In American tradition, many different forms of folk style exist, all "contaminated" by levels of culture beyond the pale of what scholars have defined as authentically traditional.

Richard M. Dorson, perhaps the most important influence on academic folklorists, an important figure in Indiana University's folklore program and a prolific writer in the field,[1] presented a major description of the folk canon and what it excluded in an article in the *American Mercury* in 1950. Dorson was anxious to underscore the conservative elements in the folklore equation, in both a technical and a political sense, and mounted a polemic against what he ingeniously called "fakelore." The neologism quickly caught on in folklore circles though its connotations were often not very clear. Dorson first defined it to mean "a synthetic product claiming to be authentic oral tradition but actually tailored for mass edification."[2] Dorson attacked "the growing popularization, commercialization, and resulting distortion of folk materials, as exemplified in the growing shelf of Paul Bunyan books and the treasuries of Ben Botkin," sources he called "fanciful whimsies" created to respond to "romantic-nationalist tendencies in the American ethos after World War I." Dorson claimed that Botkin's *A Treasury of American Folklore* (1944) and the regional compilations Botkin later issued "shaped the general conception of American folklore to this day" (5). Dorson then pointedly distinguished between "properly documented oral folklore collected directly in the field from the tellers of the tales and singers of the folksongs, and the rewritten, saccharine versions of fakelore."

> On the side of fakelore I placed the treasuries [of Botkin], Paul Bunyan books, and children's story collections, and charged that the authors, editors, and publishers had misled and gulled the public. These parlor folklorists did no fieldwork, adapted printed sources that were themselves suspect, invented out of whole cloth, emphasized the jolly, cute, and quaint, and contrived a picture of American folksiness wholly fake to social reality. (5–6)

Dorson's insistence on accurate documentation and the importance of field work is a position clearly beyond dispute. But, as Alan Dundes has emphasized, "Dorson's repeated excoriations of fakelore as well as of those who produced it often bordered on near-manic acerbic expressions of vitriol." Dundes has argued that Dorson failed to recognize the connection between fakelore and the "famous or rather infamous" Ossian poems of James Macpherson.[3] Even though the Ossianic poems were clear frauds perpetrated on an unsuspecting public, they stimulated, as Dundes has pointed out, "an interest in the poetry of the common man throughout Europe. . . . The possibility of eliciting oral poetry from the Scottish Highlands meant that epic poetry could come not just from the ancients, but also from modern, untutored peasants." With other sources, the poems inspired the study of folklore as an academic field (43–44). Moreover, Dundes has observed, Dorson seemed unaware that the versions of tales collected and heavily edited by the Grimm brothers, *Kinder und Hausmärchen* of 1812 and 1815, were also "doctored"; they were not taken, as the Grimms had claimed, from the lips of peasants. "The Grimms' offenses included disguising their actual sources and even destroying all of their original field notes," Dundes has asserted. "[F]olklorists have tended on the whole to gloss over these facts, preferring instead to continue to extol the Grimms as shining exemplars of folklore scholarship" (44–45). Finally, Dundes has claimed, Dorson overlooked the fakelore status of the *Kalevala* (1835). Created largely through the efforts of Elias Lönnrot, the *Kalevala* has been called a Finnish national epic. Dorson identified Lönnrot as "the prime figure in the illustrious record of the Finns" who "journeyed to East Karelia in the 1830s to meet singers of ancient Finnish poetry, from whose runes he stitched together the *Kalevala*" (38). But as the *Kalevala* is in fact what one scholar has termed "a composite epic, so also are the poems in it composite poems; no one song has ever been recited by the people the way it appears in the *Kalevala.*" A well-known Finnish folklorist has called it "a clear counterfeit."[4]

Dorson's willingness to accept the work of classic folklore researchers while rejecting contemporary instances of similar activity is partly due to his strong sense that the folk process works differently in the present than it did in the past. He has written, "The discovery that unlettered country people possessed their own oral literature and inherited lore, *traceable perhaps to the mental outlook of prehistoric man,* excited the new genus of folklorists" [my italics] (10). It took Dorson a long time to come around to the notion that folklore exists abundantly in the modern world, and even then he tended to identify these products as survivals of older materials rather than fresh creations. Fakelore all too easily becomes a category for anything a folklorist doesn't like or understand.

Dorson was furiously opposed to admitting into the folk canon what have come to be known as revival materials—that is, conscious attempts to conserve and develop older modes of expression. "The folklorist sets himself as a primary task separating out the folktales from the literary writings, the folksongs from the art songs, the folk art from the fine art, the folk custom and usage from the formal institutions of society, the folk speech from the standard language, the folk wisdom from the science," he has stated. "Since the lines of demarcation are frequently blurred and fuzzy, the folklorist must continually sharpen his concepts, refine his techniques, appraise his results" (11). It is just this separation between folk and all other human activity that provoked Dorson to introduce the concept of fakelore, which came to designate any items or approaches that departed from his basic conception of the qualities of traditional expression.

It is no secret among folklorists that Dorson and I have fundamentally different positions and that Dorson has voiced his differences with my views often.[5] He has claimed that my book, *The Voice of the Folk: Folklore and American Literary Theory* (1972), extends the error Constance Rourke made "of confusing folklore with sub-literature."[6] He charged that I have connected Herder, Emerson, Whitman, Rourke, the Lomaxes, Ralph Ellison, and Bob Dylan "to contrive a thesis that the central achievement of American letters rests on sustenance from folk traditions" (94). Dorson has been bothered by my interest in Ben Botkin and in the "left-wing, idea-happy Alan Lomax," whom he has contrasted with "right-wing, un-speculative" John Lomax, the father in this pioneering team of folklorists. He rejected my discussion of Emerson and Whitman for being "couched entirely in the literary criticism of the F. O. Matthiessen–Perry Miller–Henry Nash Smith–Leo Marx school," which, although it rightly sought to relate American writing to cultural thought and experience, again relied heavily on Constance Rourke's "error." And he has also disputed my view that Ralph Ellison offers important insights into the function of folklore in American literary expression. Dorson has claimed Ellison's own major work, *Invisible Man,* is "almost wholly devoid of black folk belief and narrative folklore elements." Dorson's charge that my work reveals "little knowledge of folklore (other than folksong and folk music) or folklorists" (95) perpetuates the unfortunate and ongoing separation between folklore and folk song. Finally, Dorson dismissed my discussion of how folk song has influenced important American writers. Dorson has insisted, "Bluestein's efforts to associate Ellison and Cleaver, Eliot and Joyce, James and Fitzgerald, Emerson and Whitman with 'folk ideology' carry little weight because he never relates them—if it were possible—to the body of field-collected American folklore" (96).[7]

Dorson's avowed commitment to the idea that the folklorist must scrupulously avoid ideological positions is belied by his reaction to my work, and his counsel that folklorists steer a course between the extremes of major political commitments in fact puts him squarely in an ideological camp. During the sixties Dorson vociferously debated "New Left," "radical historians" who, he charged, "sought to rewrite history from the bottom up." Dorson and other academic folklorists quickly became identified with the establishment at such academic meetings as the one where, according to Dorson, "one black-shirted radical interrupted the presidential address and attempted to take over the podium" (23).

Dorson has used this notion about the nonideological orientation of folklore to dispute the work of Eliot Wigginton, founder of the innovative educational techniques organized under the rubric Foxfire, and of such academics as Richard Drinnon, who Dorson claimed "savages" his *America in Legend* collection "for omitting Afro-American, Native American, and ethnic folk heroes and heroines, and for exalting the bloodthirsty Indian-killer Mike Fink as a legendary hero." Dorson concluded that Drinnon actually wanted him to tailor his folklore studies "to the existing ideology."

R. Serge Denisoff, Dorson has argued, correctly perceives the distinction between folklore and fakelore. To Denisoff, Woody Guthrie was "a unique hybrid of rural and urban cultures," a "folk entrepreneur" whose songs were never sung by dustbowl Okies and Arkies. Guthrie was, according to Dorson, "a conscious spokesman for proletarian values and a composer of 'agit-prop' songs," a performer who should not be confused with a "traditional singer" (98).[8]

But the idea that Guthrie's work won no place among the population involved in the Dust Bowl migrations (many of whom still resent the epithets Dorson uses) is less than accurate.[9] And, like many other critics, Dorson and Denisoff pass over the implications of the "unique hybrid of rural and urban cultures" that Guthrie represents. Because Guthrie was born of middle-class parents in a small Oklahoma town, academic folklorists have viewed him as inauthentic; his traditional-sounding, folk-based work cannot be folk song because it has clear authorship and lacks the requisite lower-class antecedents. From this point of view, Guthrie is obviously a "revivalist," a pernicious term that implies lack of association with the folk process. In recent times the term has been used to distinguish between rural performers who work in regional styles and urbanites who have become interested and often highly proficient in traditional elements of vocal and instrumental styles. More importantly, urban performers are also usually composers in folk style who, like Guthrie, often adapt traditional tunes and texts. Almost all of Guthrie's influential songs were based on variations of standard folk and popular tunes, including such widely accepted songs as "This Land Is Your Land." In my view, Guthrie's approach is not essentially different from Dan Emmett's, or from Stephen Foster's, or from that of dozens of blues performers such as Robert Johnson who have been only sketchily identified. The union parodies of church hymns by "Wobbly" composer-singer Joe Hill are also poplore.

Revival performers and composers are usually contrasted with major "folk" artists in our time, whose rural backgrounds and appropriate provenances have masked creative efforts and hybrid sources identical to those Guthrie's career illustrates. All the notable figures of twentieth-century folk fame (including white rural singers and black blues people) are actually poplorists. The main folk styles of the United States were already codified in the period after the Civil War, when the many rich strains of expression began a full interaction. Grounded in a kind of double helix of black and white source material, these tunes, rhythms, texts, and vernacular styles (especially the blues) have been the basis for all musical developments since. They have been copied, extended, and often, like bluegrass, totally re-invented by such talented and creative poplorists as Guthrie.[10]

Since the turn of the century, recordings (one of the main sources of syncretism), radio, television, and the increased mobility of artists have contributed to folk development in this country, and today it can legitimately be claimed that all major "folk" figures have been influenced strongly by popular and commercial elements. But folklorists simply have not attended to the range of their expression. They have routinely excised popular elements from their studies and have otherwise conformed their "informants" to the preconceptions already ingrained in the academic approach. Folklorists' treatment of Buell Kazee is a case in point. Kazee was a Kentucky banjoist whose fifty-two Brunswick recordings in the late 1920s were a tremendous instrumental and repertorial influence on such later performers as Pete Seeger and others. Kazee was often described as the "aboriginal Southern Appalachian folksinger," but he was actually a university-trained singer who kept his two voice styles carefully compartmentalized; New York recording specialists urged him to sound more countrified.[11] I never met a banjo picker or fiddler in the field who did not play marches or sing popular tunes, and Kazee was no exception. The non-folk sources simply never turned up on the recordings or in the printed studies.[12]

Poplorists such as Guthrie have been the most important figures in bringing together the musical and ideological implications of folk and popular culture in our time. The work of such figures as Pete Seeger and Jean Ritchie is best understood in this same framework. No one has been more instrumental in transmitting materials from folk tradition to popular audiences than Seeger, whose career defines perfectly the idea of poplore. His mother, Constance Edson Seeger, was a concert violinist; his father Charles was one of the founding fathers of ethnomusicology, a discipline that attempts to bring anthropology and musicology together. Charles's second wife, Ruth Crawford Seeger, was a collector as well as arranger of folk song materials.[13] Ruth and Charles collaborated on the music for the Lomaxes' influential study, *Folk Song: U. S. A.*

Although brought up in an intellectual milieu, Pete Seeger became intrigued by folk tradition.

> In 1935 I was sixteen years old, playing tenor banjo in the school jazz band. I was less interested in studying the classical music that my parents taught at Julliard. But my father is a musicologist, and it was through him that I first got interested in American folk music and became conscious of the immensity of the field. In 1935 a good deal of song collecting was being done under the auspices of different government agencies . . . My father, as an expert in several branches of musical scholarship, was involved in these projects. And I accompanied him on one field trip to North Carolina. We wound down through the narrow valleys with so many turns in the road that I got seasick. We passed wretched little cabins with half-naked children peering out the door; we passed exhibits of patchwork quilts and other handicrafts which often were the main source of income. . . . At the Asheville square dance and ballad festival I fell in love with the old-fashioned five-string banjo, rippling out a rhythm to one fascinating song after another. I liked the melodies, time-tested by generations of singers. I liked the words.[14]

Like many performers in poplore tradition, Seeger augmented his field work with significant innovations of his own. He discovered that old-time performers often "knew only a few tunes apiece, and maybe only one method of strumming, which they picked up from their father or a neighbor." Seeger learned the two main approaches to playing, frailing and finger-picking. But in the process of adapting the instrument to a variety of song traditions, both national and international, he invented a number of new approaches that were widely imitated. Early on he began to produce a series of instruction books, at first mimeographed and later formally published. One can almost always tell whether a player has learned from older musicians or from Seeger by the approach taken to a basic strum, the use of the first or second finger in frailing, or the preference for an unusually long-necked instrument; Seeger favored the last because it gave him greater flexibility in using the open tunings characteristic of five-string banjo style.[15]

By the 1950s, when Seeger's prolific Folkways Records output had become widely known and the Weavers singing group, of which he was part, had achieved international recognition, the five-string banjo was being produced by major companies and played by thousands of people throughout the world, often in the traditional styles Seeger reintroduced in his books honoring older folk artists and in publications offering new variations.[16] As is the case with the folk instruments of many modern nations, the five-string banjo was in danger of becoming obsolete. "For many years," Seeger has noted, " the five-string banjo was almost forgotten: instrument companies stopped making them; a hock shop was the most likely place to find one. Still it was played by back-country people, especially in the South, to accompany ballads and play for square dances." Seeger championed the instrument, which began to bring it back into circulation. When he became nationally and internationally known in the late 1940s and 1950s. he sparked a revival of the five-string banjo all around the world.[17] The instrument was saved from extinction.

Perhaps the main mark of America's folk development is the revival of such traditional instruments as the banjo, autoharp, blues harmonica, fiddle, and mountain dulcimer by young performers who often take their inspiration from a poplorist like Seeger and whose own work creates further variations in traditional styles.[18] In her survey of the banjo's image in popular culture, Karen Linn has concluded, "Once plantation black, then mountain white, the five-string banjo now invites the children of late twentieth century

America (primarily the white children) onto the mountain porch . . . to partake of the musical moment, to experience the not quite tamed wildness within, and to construct (if only for a weekend) a sense of authenticity—an authenticity that springs from the sentimental values of American culture."[19] Linn has recognized Seeger's crucial role in popularizing the instrument, but she has not caught the way he understood the banjo. From his earliest performances, Seeger used it to unify black and white materials. During the civil rights movement of the 1960s, Seeger's banjo brought black materials to a nation and conveyed his insistence that the country could survive only with "black and white together." Historically, the banjo symbolized either outrageous black stereotypes or genteel parlor materials.[20] Seeger's approach was an impressive turnabout: his long-necked instrument became finally a central symbol of integration.[21] Nothing, of course, was more appropriate for an instrument whose history has been determined by both black and white influences.

To Dorson, Guthrie and Seeger were "socialist-singers" rejected by the labor groups they had hoped to influence. The truth in this comment is unassailable. But even as the labor movement showed a general lack of sustained interest in the music both preserved and created for them by such politically oriented groups as the Almanac Singers,[22] the influence of Seeger and others permeated a much broader social and political spectrum.[23] The American labor movement is after all a peculiarly middle-class phenomenon. And when big business has exerted unbearable pressure on American workers, they have become noticeably interested in labor songs, picket line ditties, and songs of solidarity.[24]

Seeger's approach moves along the lines of the radical egalitarianism, humane nationalism, and profound international vision Herder articulated, though Seeger himself has always acknowledged the influence of Marxism on his ideas. Herder's legacy is perhaps more plainly visible in the civil rights movement, in which songs (especially from black tradition) became the mainstay of activities that without them might not have succeeded. It was Herder not Marx who predicted that folklore would define the outlines of a nation's culture and, as we have seen, the Herderian model clarifies the multicultural aspect of our tradition. Not only the movement's anthem, "We Shall Overcome," but dozens of other variations adapted in poplore style from folklore shored up the political activity of civil rights activists and spilled over into the mass media. Seeger and others adapted "We Shall Overcome" from a union song based on a black spiritual.[25] Seeger and Lee Hays, his longtime collaborator and Weavers colleague, composed "If I Had a Hammer," which gave clear meanings to the traditional values of American egalitarianism and the idea that music has the power to unite the nation.

Many songs by Seeger and other poplorists have moved along the same political and cultural lines, adapting folk motifs to broader and often overtly political concerns. The list is longer than I can recount here, but it includes Seeger's widely received "Where Have All the Flowers Gone," "Turn, Turn, Turn," "Whimoweh" (his adaptation of a South African freedom song), "Waist Deep In the Big Muddy"; Guthrie's "This Land Is Your Land" (which many have proposed as a new national anthem),[26] "Pastures of Plenty," and "So Long It's Been Good to Know You," not to mention his many children's songs, which influenced several generations of young people and their parents. One should also mention here the work of Malvina Reynolds, whose songs "Little Boxes" (it put the term "ticky-tacky" in the dictionary), "What Have They Done to the Rain," "God Bless the Grass," and many others have been strong influences on a "greening" tradition in our time.

While Seeger has often used his popularity to bring such traditional musicians as Leadbelly and Sonny Terry to the attention of large audiences, his own special talents have usually been overlooked. Like Macpherson, the Grimms, and Lönnrot, Seeger developed special skills in relation to folk material, talents that we have not examined closely and for which we have developed no name. Yet those abilities, secondary as they may be, have major implications for the field of modern folk research. Dan Emmett and many little-known American performers have shown similar talents. Though a trained musician, Seeger consciously schooled himself in folk arts by studying traditional modes of expression and using them in his own creative framework. Sometimes the results are so close to folk style that they could be easily passed off as authentic, but Seeger has always acknowledged his sources. He has researched and written about most of the major folk traditions of interest in our time, among them traditional ballads, the twelve-string guitar, the five-string banjo, and the steel drums of Trinidad.[27]

The problem Seeger presents to conventional students of folk tradition is that they know who he is, just as they can identify Guthrie as a composer. Despite the fact that their songs have been appropriated by masses of people and have begun to undergo the variations characteristic of the folk process, the criterion of anonymity has placed their work in a category that cannot even be discussed or that carries the label fakelore.

But as anthropologist Sally Price has recently shown in a provocative study of primitive art, the notion of universality reflects great condescension toward its creators.

> The Family of Man encompasses not only brotherhood but also sibling rivalry, and the recognition of shared concerns or pleasures coexists and competes with an insistence on those essential features that separate the Civilized and Primitive branches of the genealogy. The Noble Savage and the Pagan Cannibal are in effect a single figure, described by a distant Westerner in two different frames of mind: portrayals of Primitive Man can be tilted either way in their recognition that he is at once a "brother" and an "other." The imagery used to convey Primitive Artists' otherness employs a standard rhetoric of fear, darkness, pagan spirits, and eroticism.[28]

Price has cited Leo Stein's ideas about the basis of our interest in the primitive—it comes from an attempt to repossess a lost innocence and to "regain a sense of seeing with the uneducated gaze of the savage and childlike eye" (33). What engaged western sensibilities was the primitive object, not the artist. "In the Western understanding of things," Price has explained, "a work originating outside of the Great Traditions must have been produced by an unnamed figure who represents his community and whose craftsmanship respects the dictates of its age-old traditions." But Price has identified a countervailing trend among some anthropologists, among them Franz Boas, who insisted that scholarly attention be paid to "the play of imagination and the role of virtuosity."

> His students, who dominated a whole generation of American anthropology, carried on these concerns through research that treated

the interplay of tradition and creativity as a matter for careful empirical investigation rather than logical deduction; their efforts began to
put on record the degree to which individual non-Western artists
could implement conscious, and sometimes innovative, aesthetic
choices within the broad outlines of the artistic traditions in which
they were trained. As a result, readers of Ruth Bunzel's study of
Pueblo pottery became familiar not only with the characteristics of
Zuni, Acoma, Hopi, and San Ildefonso styles, but also with the more
individualized attributes of the work of potters such as Maria Mar-
tinez and Nampeyo. (57)

As scholars begin to break down the stereotypes of primitive artists as faceless, unconscious naifs, folklorists should recognize
that anonymity is no longer an essential prerequisite of folk expression. Folklorists have been too committed to dogma to comprehend the message of the blues tag, "If anyone asks you who composed this song, / Tell him it was Huddie Ledbetter, he's been here
and gone." Leadbelly didn't make up the song, but, like most artists, he wrote himself into it in many subtle ways.

In the United States, folk expression has continued in the framework of poplore and without prejudice to the recognition of authorship. As Price has pointed out, "A case can be made that the 'anonymity' (and its corollary, the 'timelessness') of Primitive Art owes
much to the needs of Western observers to feel that their society
represents a uniquely superior achievement in the history of humanity" (60). It was just such patronizing attitudes toward folklore
that prompted Herder to propose "the equal validity of incommensurable cultures," and Lévi-Strauss to argue that the differences
between mythic (*sauvage*) and contemporary modes of thought
are of degree and not of kind. Folk and formal arts are a continuum,
not a disjunction. Recognizing the legitimacy of contemporary artists in folk frameworks not only broadens our understanding of
human creativity; it ensures that folk processes will continue to
enrich our culture as well.

Consider as a final example of poplore the work of Kentuckian
Jean Ritchie. Unlike Seeger, Ritchie comes from a traditional community in the Cumberland mountains. Born in Viper, Kentucky, in
1922, the youngest in a family of fourteen children, she graduated
from the University of Kentucky with highest honors and as a mem-

ber of Phi Beta Kappa. Ritchie then worked as a social worker in New York's Henry Street Settlement House. Alan Lomax recorded her for the Library of Congress and introduced her to Oxford University Press, which originally published her now-classic work about her life in the mountains, *Singing Family of the Cumberlands.*

Ritchie grew up in a singing family and learned to play the three-stringed Appalachian dulcimer, a plucked psaltery which has a number of European analogues. Her brilliant memoir of life on the family farm recalls the evening sessions when the family would move to the porch. "I remember I would always be so afraid that the family would decide *not* to sing tonight, that I would even dry the dishes without being made to. I would keep talking all the while about what a pretty time it was outside, to get them in the notion."[29] Ritchie used to try to get her father, a fine singer, fiddler, and dulcimer player, to talk about the old days, and in one of these conversations he told her when he first heard a fiddle played: "He was a little slip of a boy, he said, about nine years old, and he was going to school to old man Nick Gerhart. . . . when Maggard Richard came in. 'He'd been off somewheres, courting in Virginny and had brought a feller home with him . . . But you know that stranger had a fiddle in his hand, first one any of us had ever seen . . . Lordie! I thought that was the prettiest sweepingest music. . . . I just couldn't mortally stand to sit still on that log bench and that tune snakin' around' " (45).

Ritchie's father had made a gourd fiddle, but she never learned to play the instrument. She instead became proficient on the dulcimer, also made by hand in the mountains then. She recalls well the coming of the railroad to her part of Kentucky and how it brought with it songs from the black repertoire, such as "John Henry."[30] And Ritchie also remembered the radio:

> We heard about the radio for a long time before we ever saw one, but the day that my brother Raymond brought one in home, that was a day we all remember. . . . Pauline and Jewel were crazy about the songs they heard through the earphones, and they had to listen and learn them and sing them so we could tell whether we liked them or not. . . . Hillbilly songs the radio called this music, and it claimed that these songs were sung all through the mountains, but we never had

heard anything like them before. I guess if it hadn't been for the radio it's no telling how long it would have taken us to find out that we were hillbillies, or what kind of songs we were supposed to sing. (248)

Between the radio and the phonograph, Ritchie recalled, there was little singing in the family. People began to feel self-conscious about the old songs. Ritchie remembered a man saying to her, " 'Barbry Ellen'? Why folks laugh at you if you sing that old thing. Call you a 'hillbilly.' And then he'd sing 'After the Ball Is Over,' a high-class song, a city song."[31] Ritchie admitted similar feelings. "In my mind the songs all got mixed and tangled until I came to think on the hillbilly songs and the old songs as the same kind of thing, got ashamed to be caught singing either kind, got to liking the slick city music on the radio the best, and I guess most everybody did likewise. Anyway, I remember a time, some few years there, when we in our family didn't near sing our own songs like we used to" (249).[32] But the radio and the phonograph had simply broadcast the mixture of folk elements that had been a feature of American life from the beginning. Radio and recording were in fact the principal vehicles for the continuing interaction of white and black traditions.[33]

But Ritchie was only briefly daunted by the popular music the radio and phonograph had introduced to her world. When she first began to perform, the mountain dulcimer, like the five-string banjo, was close to extinction; without her popularizing influence, the dulcimer today would be little more than a museum artifact. But the circumstances in which Ritchie performed inspired her to make some important changes in the instrument. In order to get a little more volume from what is essentially a sweet (dulcet) and quiet instrument, she used a model about a third larger than the smaller instruments made in her area.[34] She also added an additional high string, though the extra string had no impact on her noting or strumming style: traditionally, the left hand employs a wooden noter and the right hand strums with a turkey feather.

As she adapted her family repertoire to performance situations, Ritchie also began to finger-pick with her right hand. This approach allowed her to create stunning countermelodies of a kind never heard in traditional dulcimer style.[35] As Pete Seeger had done with the five-string banjo, Jean Ritchie had made basic and influential changes in the approach to the traditional instrument. Again like Seeger, Ritchie began early in her career to issue instruction books and demonstration recordings, which resulted in a worldwide revival of interest in the dulcimer. By Dorson's standards, this "interference" is fakelore. But Ritchie in fact made an extraordinary and disciplined contribution to the survival of an important aspect of our cultural heritage while she distinguished herself as a remarkable performer.

Like many poplorists, Ritchie has often written new texts to old tunes or has introduced interesting variations on both tune and text. She has never changed her style of performing the secular and religious tunes she grew up with. She sings many of them a cappella and others in "hillbilly" style, with guitar or autoharp accompaniment. This latter style recalls the influence of such groups as the Carter Family, whose records and radio appearances left a deep impression on many who heard them. Even more than fellow Kentuckian Buell Kazee, who knew how to turn his concert voice off and on according to the repertoire, Ritchie has shown over more than fifty years that a consciousness of responsibility to an inherited repertoire can resist the impact of commercial styles. Poplore, represents a deep and very delicate balance between traditional and selected popular styles that, in the hands of less devoted artists, can result in an overwhelming of the folk elements rather than the syncretism of poplore.[36]

Working with traditional forms and language, Ritchie has composed a number of songs so folk in quality that they are widely accepted as traditional. These include a number of protest songs that deal with the hardships of miners and their families, people she knows well from her Kentucky girlhood. Several were published under the pseudonym 'Than Hall (after her maternal grandfather, Jonathan) in order to protect her Kentucky family from the anger of coal companies. She has heard from many people that they knew this composer and can testify to the authenticity of his background and the accuracy of his perceptions.[37]

Karen Linn has suggested that the dulcimer was associated with "the romanticized time of the 'old stock's' ancestors." While the banjo had "a wildness that threatened the nobler aspects of mountain culture and the sanctity of the home, [the] dulcimer is always shown at home, and usually played by a woman, the representative of domesticity."[38] The dulcimer supposedly cemented the connection between the alleged prestigious Elizabethan traditions and a Southern mountain locale not always depicted so positively. (In fact, the dulcimer has no British antecedents whatsoever, its main analogues found in Germany and Norway.) But Ritchie's poploristic instincts have led her away from the status quo; instead, she has used her dulcimer as part of an argument for freedom and economic justice.

# Conclusion

"There are always two parties, the party of the Past and the party of the Future; the Establishment and the Movement," Emerson once wrote. "At times the resistance is reanimated, the schism runs under the world and appears in Literature, Philosophy, Church, State and social customs."[1] The dialectic between the past and the future was evident during the generational conflict of the 1960s, when a sometimes strange coalition of young people committed to everything from civil rights to unlimited and instant gratification stripped away an accumulation of hypocrisy about certain basic American values.

Similarly, today's debates over multiculturalism (or pluralism), affirmative action, the revision of literary and historical canons (which some claim to constitute an attack against western civilization), and anomalously the literary philosophy called deconstruction[2] also pit certain scholars against a rear-guard movement that stubbornly refuses to acknowledge some fundamental realities of the American experience. As I have argued, our culture is already pluralist and multicultural, the result of a syncretic process that dates from the beginning of our national existence and that has colored black, essential elements of our society. Herder's ideas are central to this understanding in two ways.

First, Herder's assertion that the folk determine the national characteristics of each society could actually lead to the conclusion that the United States was not a coherent and nationally mature culture, but, as folklorists have often maintained, a callow and derivative one. Folklorists have consistently argued that our folk legacy was only what had been brought here from other more mature societies; thus, the United States is not authentically a nation at all. Dorson's conception of fakelore arises logically from such a view. The authentic folk, he has asserted, remain in the distant past; what looks like folklife today is simply fakelore, fraudulent because it is associated with known individuals whose folk credentials have been irreparably damaged by contact with popular levels of culture.

For Dorson and others, conservatism is both a methodology and an ideology that turns us to the past rather than the future. Conservatism implies slow change that retains traditional materials over long periods of time. Despite the extensive and manifold influence of such people as Woody Guthrie, Pete Seeger, and Jean Ritchie, folklorists have simply not been able to place these artists in any coherent framework. While academic critics may have grudgingly admired their work, its alleged contamination by pop traditions has put them in a sort of limbo. They have obviously done something with folk material, but what they have done is difficult to evaluate within the obsolete definitions of folklore still in vogue.

However, Herder's folk ideology helps clarify the fact that the United States is an authentic as well as a multicultural nation. As Constance Rourke and the Lomaxes have argued, our heritage of folkloristic materials represents a syncretism of remarkable extent and variety, one so varied and intertwined that it defines us unmistakably. If Old World folk activity is understood to be essentially conservative, New World folk expression is clearly forward-looking and often radical in its political and esthetic commitments.

The United States does not possess a body of anonymously created materials developed over long periods of time. What the nation has is poplore, an obvious mix of folk and pop elements that is associated with many known artists, whose esthetic contributions often change the inherited materials before our eyes. If we had more accurate information about ancient folk artists, we might discover precisely the same process at work even in early tribal societies, as Sally Price and others have suggested.

Elite culture exists in the United States, as does culture that is folk in more conventional terms. But the characteristic American experience involves a melding of folk and pop in the context of many diverse cultures, united largely by a substructure of African-American stylistic preferences. Poplore defines this unique tradition, and it unfolds in many major areas of cultural expression—as the basis of popular music from blues to rock, in literature, and in the many hybrid forms that inform American arts.[3] Herder thought his folk ideology would create a truly national but clearly middle-class culture. Poplore, on the contrary, always (if often indirectly) points to a radically egalitarian commitment that seriously undermines the racist and sexist values of bourgeois society. Mainstream folklorists such as Richard Dorson have insisted that "reform-minded" expression is not folklore. In so doing, they ignore the basically subversive element in much folk expression. Political conservatives both in and out of government have always been able to identify the radical components in these works. Like Emerson, poplorists insist that we take our democratic heritage literally and reject those elements in our history that purport to justify inequality.

Herder cannot have suspected that the internationalism he envisioned would appear so fully in one society. Both the extensive mixtures of ethnic elements in the United States and the current World Beat music scene reveal a level of international consciousness far beyond the limited, provincial awareness defined in most views of nationalism or even in Herder's enlightened conceptions. "Polyethnicity was not Herder's idea," Isaiah Berlin explains. "He didn't urge the Germans to study Dutch or German students to study the culture of the Portuguese."

Throughout much of the modern world, however, nationalist movements continue to fuel political life. As Berlin has noted, "In our modern age, nationalism is not resurgent; it never died. . . . In the twentieth century, no left-wing movement succeeded in Asia or Africa—in Indochina, Egypt, Algeria, Syria, or Iraq—unless it went arm in arm with nationalist feeling."[4] These movements do not exemplify the sort of cultural self-determination Herder described— as Berlin has put it, "a set of customs and a life style, a way of perceiving and behaving that is of value solely because it is their own." What occurred in Eastern Europe and the former Soviet Union resulted from nationalist movements already frustrated by imperialist regimes that had absorbed ancient cultures into such artificial "nations" as Yugoslavia and the USSR. But the United States, Berlin has suggested, has not experienced this "violent counterreaction."[5] "Only in America," he has stated, "have a variety of ethnic groups retained . . . some part of their own original culture and nobody seems to mind."

Berlin's naïveté is clear for we well know that ethnic tensions exist and have often exploded in tragedy and violence. A more accurate evaluation, as I have tried to show, is that ethnicity and national pride slowly but inevitably result in syncretic movements that provide just the common elements that critics of cultural pluralism fear we are losing to our peril. Commentators such as Allan Bloom have demanded a return to those elements of "Western Civilization" that multiculturalists and literary and historical revisionists are seen to have threatened. Louis Menand has argued that "the United States is becoming not more multicultural, but less. For when the whole culture is self-consciously 'diverse,' real diversity has disappeared."[6] "Real" diversity—"functionally autonomous subcultures within a dominant culture, or . . . conflicting tastes and values specifically associated with ethnicity, gender and sexual preference"—does not, Menand has asserted, exist here.

What Americans continue to have in common, however, is not the heritage of Greece and Rome but a tradition based on the combinations and hybridizations that merged African-American, Anglo-Celtic, and a dozen other sources into the patchwork quilt of the American experience—a diversity based on the syncretism I have been describing.[7] Convinced by critics over the years that the United States is a feckless and vulgar society, we now face the task of looking honestly at what has been wrought here in order to place it carefully in the context of the modern world.

# Appendix One

## Moses Asch
## and the Legacy of
## Folkways Records

None of the early inventors of the phonograph had even the vaguest notion of its ultimate cultural impact. Thomas Alva Edison was experimenting with ways of recording telegraph and telephone messages when he ran into a curious phenomenon "resembling human talk heard indistinctly."[1] He noted the results of his work on 18 July 1877: "Just tried experiment with diaphragm having an embossing point and held against paraffin paper moving rapidly. The speaking vibrations are indented nicely, and there's no doubt that I shall be able to store up and reproduce automatically at any future time the human voice perfectly." Ultimately he changed over from paraffin to tinfoil and created a metal cylinder with two needles, one of which would record and the other reproduce the sounds. A year later, Edison suggested ten ways in which the phonograph might be of use—for letter writing and dictation, talking books for the blind, aids to elocution, the reproduction of all kinds of music, recording of family histories, the creation of music boxes and toys, talking clocks, the preservation of rare languages, the recording of educational lectures, and the creation of permanent telephone messages.

But the level of technology was so low that hardly anyone took Edison's suggestions seriously. Like most potential investors, Edison himself was convinced that the main impact of his invention would be in commercial applications. As interest in the phonograph waned, Edison became interested in the possibility of an incandescent lamp, and the phonograph was largely forgotten for about ten years. Then, Alexander Graham Bell and his colleagues improved on Edison's invention with a machine they called a graphophone, which set Edison and others back on the track of the original device. Stenographers, however, violently resisted the machine because they believed it placed their profession in serious jeopardy. Whenever a business tested a phonograph in an office, Roland Gelatt has observed, "the alarmed stenographers (still predominantly male) would make sure that it developed such serious defects as to make it impracticable for their employer's use."

Despite Edison's objections, entrepreneurs began to investigate the entertainment possibilities of the phonograph. A nickel-in-the-slot version, providing short snatches of Souza marches and Stephen Foster tunes, met with great success. "The 'coin-in-the-slot' device is calculated to injure the phonograph in the opinion of those seeing it only in that form . . . as nothing more than a mere toy," Edison warned in 1891, "and no one would comprehend its value or appreciate its utility as an aid to businessmen and others for dictation purposes when seeing it only in that form."

By the mid-nineties, however, the phonograph became a fixture in the entertainment industry. Phonograph cylinders featured lectures, humorous recitations, popular songs, black impersonators, and the work of George W. Johnson, "a Negro with an infectious laugh, who became famous for his record of 'The Whistling Coon.'" In 1894 even Edison began to acknowledge the possibilities of the phonograph in entertainment. He began to plan a cheap model that ordinary Americans could afford. When Emile Berliner invented a method of duplication and a machine he called a gramophone that used discs, the cylinder's days were numbered, and the fruition of recording was imminent.

In 1904, for a fee of $4,000, Enrico Caruso recorded ten disc sides in Carnegie Hall. By 1906, Caruso was recording with an orchestra. In the early 1920s, a number of companies began to produce the recordings that ultimately became known as "Race Records," featuring blues and gospel singers and introducing such best-selling artists as Lucille Hegamin, Mamie Smith, Ma Rainey, Alberta Hunter, and the great Bessie Smith. Record companies also recruited male blues singers during field trips to the South, and soon afterward they signed white artists to record what came to be known as "hillbilly" music. The classic jazz recordings featuring such artists as King Oliver, Louis Armstrong, and Jelly Roll Morton were also produced in this decade.

The idea underlying these recordings was to develop products for groups in totally segregated enclaves—"Race Records" for blacks, "hillbilly" for whites. Cajun and a host of other more obviously ethnic recordings were also produced and marketed in this way.[2] None of the producers was aware that these field recordings had begun to limn the outlines of a major tradition of folk and pop activity in the United States. Since 1933, the Music Division of the Library of Congress has recorded all types of folk music and has assembled these recordings into an archive. Led by John A. Lomax, field workers took mobile recording units into all areas of the country, particularly to prison farms and penitentiaries. By 1942, they had amassed about four thousand titles by 850 African-American singers and scores of others.[3]

With Moses Asch and Folkways Records, the underlying multicultural implications of the recording industry took on their full meaning. For almost forty years, Moe Asch attempted to document the important events of his time through Folkways Records, and the miracle of Folkways involved more than the efficiency Asch liked to boast about. His determination to publish anything that he thought worthy of preservation (regardless of its lack of acoustic fidelity or its minimal sales potential) was backed by a hard-nosed approach to royalties for his artists. Most of the time the recording artists received an advance of about $150. A great many of the issues never sold enough to warrant anything more. But the only way to find out was to badger Asch until he looked into the accounting files, which were never kept up to date. In general, any overall profits were plowed back into the company to continue expanding the catalogue and to keep every entry in print.

At the same time, as Pete Seeger has noted, Asch kept him on a minimal payroll during the lean years when Seeger was effectively blacklisted. It is ironic that Asch ultimately was able to capitalize on the popularity of Seeger's recordings during the heyday of the folk boom in the sixties and seventies. Despite the great variety of materials that Asch was willing to publish, there's no doubt that the most important effect of his work was to make available an incredible range of worldwide traditional materials.

The existence of those materials, in turn, stimulated the development of all the newer approaches by artists whom I have described as poplorists, from Seeger and Guthrie to Dylan and the many rock musicians who used older traditional materials, especially the heritage of blues singers and instrumentalists. Because of Asch's devotion, it was possible for anyone to study the great traditions of our heritage or almost any other in the world just by buying a record or taking it out of the local library. As recordings had been one of the important vehicles for integrating the styles of American artists from early times (recordings of Native Americans had appeared as early as the 1890s), so the availability of the rich legacy of our traditional culture was accelerated by the Folkways enterprise.

Almost the whole tradition of what we call rock and roll has its roots in the mix of materials that took place through the agency of records—whites listening to blues, blacks listening to the traditions evolved from their own sources, as well as Anglo-Celtic ones. At the same time, an ethnic element shows up in such curious developments as the adoption of the German accordion tradition in the music of Louisiana Cajuns, itself (with its black counterpart, Zydeco) a mixing of Anglo-Celtic, French, and African sources. Nothing is more germane than the revival of Klezmer music, the traditions of Jewish east European village music, almost obliterated by the Holocaust but preserved largely through American recordings and recently the subject of a major American revival.[4] In these and many other instances, Folkways recordings provided both the traditional materials and the poploristic sources of many contemporary musical ideas. The rich catalogue is far from having exhausted its potential for influencing future developments.

Among the many effects of Asch's work, not the least is a major correction of the notion that technological development spells the end of folk arts. What is clear from the Folkways experience is that recordings helped to preserve the important traditions, some of which were in real danger of extinction, and also provided the resources for the new developments that characterize contemporary poplore activity. The result has been basically different from the folk expression of the past; as Asch's history reveals, there is extensive intervention from nonfolk sources in the creation of some of our most interesting materials. Charles Seeger pointed out the same fact many years ago.

The avidity of the hillbilly most remote from the city for the city's nonfolkness is quite as self-propelled as that of the city-billy most remote from the country for the country's folkness. Since each has now exploited the other for a couple of decades in the large frame of the United States, there must exist few, if any, persons left ratable as 100 percent either folk or nonfolk. The vast population lies between these limits, each individual made up of varying proportions of inhibited or released folkness or nonfolkness. Perhaps we could venture some definitions now, as, for example, "nonfolkness is that which tries not to be folkness"; "folkness is that which knows of no more nonfolkness that it can try to be." The possibility cannot but occur to one that perhaps the two are not mutually exclusive opposites but overlapping complements or, perhaps two aspects of one unbroken continuum.[5]

The work of individuals such as Asch and the many others who contributed to the collection and distribution of recorded materials accelerated a process initiated by many other elements of a syncretic nature.

The story of how Folkways was organized has become a kind of folktale for which a number of variants exist, all of them involving a meeting with Albert Einstein. Folksong collector and author Samuel Charters has offered one version: "Folkways Records was actually planned at an evening conversation with Moe Asch, his father, and Albert Einstein, who was a friend of Moe's father. Moe commented that he would like to have a record com-

pany 'to describe the human race, the sound it makes, what it creates.'
Moe was very young. And Einstein said, 'I think that's a good idea.'"

I asked Moe Asch what he remembered about the circumstances of the
company's creation.

The second World War was on. People in Europe didn't know how the
U.S. stands. We didn't take sides. The Jewish committee here decided that they would broadcast the thought and ideas of famous
Jews in America so that they shouldn't feel in Europe that these
people that left ran away here and left them holding the bag. The rich
especially were able to buy passage and live here like kings. Over
there they were being beaten and killed by the Germans, and there
was a lot of anti-Semitic feeling in England and elsewhere that these
refugees have no right to come here and take our bread and butter
away—just like the Jamaicans in England. The committee decided
who the great Jews in America were, and one of them was Einstein.
The committee knew of me and my work with the International Ladies Garment Workers Union, and they knew I was in this business of
recording, but they didn't know how to approach Einstein. But since
he was a good friend of Father's, it was easy for me to go to Princeton
and record him. And he did four broadcasts. When he couldn't do
them live, we made an acetate record to be broadcast later. That's
how I came to be with Einstein. Then Einstein asked me what I was
doing, and I told him. By that time I had recorded Leadbelly and a
number of other American folk things, Yiddish folk songs, the Bagelman Sisters, Ukrainians. And I explained my theory of documentation and what I wanted to do and what I thought my future was. He
said I should stick to this because in Europe all that was being wiped
out and here it was being assimilated. I brought some albums and
showed them to him. He said the same thing as my father.[6]

Asch's father was the Yiddish writer, Sholem Asch, born in 1860 in the
little town of Kutno, about seventy-five miles west of Warsaw in what was
then Polish-Russia. His early work was discovered by the classic Yiddish
writer, I. L. Peretz, who encouraged Asch to write in Yiddish rather than in
Hebrew. From almost the beginning, Asch's nonconformity and modernism
embroiled him in protracted controversy, culminating in accusations of
apostasy when in 1939 he published a fictional life of Christ, *The Nazarene*.
But Asch's scandalous behavior began even earlier when he wrote *God of
Vengeance* (mounted by Max Reinhardt in 1910). A play involving prostitu-
tion and lesbianism, it was severely criticized, especially for a scene in
which a Torah is placed in a brothel. But Reinhardt's Berlin production

brought early recognition to the author. Peretz and other literary friends had advised Asch to destroy the play, but he rejected all entreaties to curtail his crusading temperament. Until his final years, which were spent in Israel, Asch consistently strove to keep his writing in the mainstream of modern literary practices. As a result, his life was in constant turmoil. He engaged in a lifelong debate with critics who opposed his attempts to unite Jewish and Christian traditions in a series of fictional works that included *The Apostle* (1943), *Mary* (1949), and *Moses* (1951). Like Edmund Wilson, whose investigations of the Dead Sea Scrolls led him to similar ecumenical conclusions, Asch encountered angry objections from both Jewish and Christian sources.

Moe Asch (pronounced like the word *ash*) was the second son of Sholem Asch (rhymes with posh).

**Asch:** I was born in Warsaw, Poland, December 2, 1905. All the children were born in Warsaw—me, two brothers, and a sister. My older brother, Nathan, became a well-known writer, the author of a controversial book called *Pay Day* [1930]; my younger brother is an agriculturalist, and my sister Ruth lives in London; Nathan is dead. We lived in Warsaw for maybe a year after I was born. I remember that we moved to Berlin when I was a baby, and I can still recall the white suit that I wore when we lived there. Reinhardt agreed to do father's *God of Vengeance* in 1910 in Berlin, and that was why we left Poland because father had to be there while the production was put on. But there was trouble between Russia, Poland, and Germany, so he never went back, and soon his income on royalties stopped. So he came to America to write and lecture. He traveled all over and wrote an article every Thursday for Abraham Cahan at the Jewish Daily *Forward.* He got twenty-five dollars a week. We children were in Paris because they didn't want to disrupt our education. When World War I was declared, Father and Mother called us in to New York, and we got here in late August. The war broke out August 1, 1914. We came with my Aunt Bashe [Barbara Spiro]—you can read about her as well as my mother in Father's novel *Three Cities* [1933]; the section on Warsaw is the life of my mother. My grandfather was the only one who defied the Polish-Russian regime. He had the only Yiddish school in Warsaw that also taught Polish rather than Russian. My mother was a teacher there—she was all of eighteen or nineteen. Grandfather was killed in the Holocaust. My Aunt Bashe, Mother's sister, took care of us later. She was an organizer, a staunch Communist who later became an important adviser to Lenin. She was always in trouble with the authorities, who tried to send her to Siberia, but she always managed to escape. Of course, anyone who went to Siberia never came back. She became Lenin's adviser on early childhood education. She was one of the first pupils of Montessori and set up childcare centers for Lenin.

I remember very well the day the Russian Revolution was declared. My aunt was a registered nurse and she was working at Montefiore Hospital in New York and she called me in that day and said, "I have to go back, the revolution is on." She stayed and married, and her daughter is an engineer there.

Father and Mother spoke Yiddish to each other; we spoke to them in the language of the period. When we were in Paris we spoke French to them; when we were in America we spoke English to them. My mother tried to teach me Yiddish when I was seven, but I never got on to it even though she was a good teacher. Later when I studied in Germany I had a hard time because of the little Yiddish I knew. *Three Cities* was based on Grandfather's life as Father saw it. He met my mother when he came from his *shtetl,* his town was Kutno, and he wrote a story called "The Little Town." I. L. Peretz saw the story and said, "This young man has talent." My father was seventeen at the time, and Peretz called him to Warsaw. In Warsaw under Peretz there started to gather the literary intellects, the first Jewish movement in Yiddish. Father wrote all his life in Yiddish, except for a few brief articles. But he did a recording for me in English, the story of the birth of Christ, the Nativity, as he interpreted it. But otherwise he wrote in Yiddish and always in longhand. In New York he was earning twenty-five dollars a week, and he couldn't write in our apartment—we lived in the Bronx. And he couldn't live in a Jewish neighborhood because the neighbors would bother him, so we had to live in a house outside those areas. And Mother took care of him. He decided that when the children reached the age of seventeen he couldn't support them anymore. He told us very early: "At the age of seventeen, you're out." Then when he became quite wealthy with *The Nazarene*—that was in the early forties—it was different. He was more secure, and we were able to talk to each other as human beings. Before that we were children, and there couldn't be any real communication. We hated our childhood. Everything had to be still, you couldn't move, you couldn't talk, you couldn't whisper because Father was always working. They beat us because the dog would turn things over and mess up the house. We had a rough time as kids. We were happy when they went away on trips to Palestine and other places. Our aunt took care of us then, my Aunt Bashe; she was a great person.

**Bluestein:** What happened when you came to the United States?

**A:** As I said, I came to this country in August of 1914. Father was already here with Mother and my sister, and I came with my two brothers and my aunt. We lived in the Bronx, next door to Leon Trotsky, who was my father's friend, and we moved from there to Brooklyn. This was in 1917, and I was twelve years old. The people next door were radio hams, and immediately my imagination started to work. This was before the end of World War I. We had no radio tubes in those days. They had a spark for transmission. No voice was used; it was just code. And I became involved in the radio with the chap next door, because I saw the possibility, coming from Europe where there were only boundaries, that this was a medium that overcame boundaries, overcame customs. The air was free. We were able to communicate all over the world with other human beings without any barriers. That was my introduction to electronics. In April of 1917 when we entered the war, the government stopped all broadcasting, all wireless, and so we had to dismantle the equipment. And you weren't allowed to have a receiver. So I stopped in this area. Then we moved to Staten Island, and I went to public school and graduated. I became one of the first organizers of the Staten Island radio club. This is around 1919. And I became very involved with transmission; I had call letters and had communication all over the world.

**B:** Did your father continue to travel?

**A:** Yes, in 1922 Father was back in Europe, and he wrote me and said, "Listen, there is an inflation going on here, and I can put you through college for a dollar a day in Germany. Take with you 300 dollars in single bills so every day you'll change as the money changes, and you'll pay your tuition and board and everything else." So what was I going to do in Germany? I didn't know any German. He lived in Koblenz and that was on the Rhine and that was occupied by American troops; after the first year they left, and the French took over. I went to this school—it was a *Hochschule,* which is like a community, technical college—to study electronics, without a damn word of German and only the lousy Yiddish, which got in my way every time I tried to speak German. But anyway I understood what they were trying to say. I worked with a professor who built the first radio transmitter during the war in Berlin, and he was working in high frequency in those days. We had an interesting time because this being the Rhine it was an international school. The Dutch from the upper Rhine came down, Russians—all kinds of students. That's when I first started to hear about folk music. And the first thing I heard was that there isn't any folk music in America, just a wilderness with Indians in the streets. It was during that time that I picked up my first book about folk music by John Lomax. One day when I was in Paris on vacation from school, browsing through the bookstalls along the Seine, I came across the 1913 edition of John Lomax's cowboy ballads [*Cowboy Songs and Frontier Ballads*], and it had an introduction by Teddy Roosevelt which guided me through life because he said that folklore and folk songs were the real expression of a people's culture.[7] And when I got back I was able to show the kids at school that there was a uniqueness in our culture. It was not just a melting pot. Lomax showed clearly that there was a folklore in America. All this stayed in the back of my mind; I didn't do anything about it until the thirties when I got through with my electronic business and I wanted to go on my own. But I learned a great deal about electronics and logic and organization. That's what the Germans knew very well—that one and one has to come out two.

**B:** What was your electronics business?

**A:** I came back to the United States in 1926. I had an inkling of electronics and I had a theory and I knew that my theory was right because it was based on logic. Those were the days when you had to use logic to refute the textbooks, because if you followed the textbooks of the time they stopped you. I found out that the exceptions were the rule. So I utilized this knowledge because I had to be on my own—as I told you, Father kicked us out at the age of seventeen. First I went to RCA. I met Mr. Sarnoff, who was a friend of Father's, and he said, "No Jew should be in radio or electronics. Get the hell out of here. This is no place for you. If you want to sell, I'll give you a job." I said, "I'm not interested in selling. I'm an engineer." From there I went to Lee De Forest in New Jersey and built with him transformers as the manager of his plant. And I set up the testing equipment. In those days we had the first television disc, and I saw the first television broadcasts of the telephone company. I was then involved with the Radio Industry Association. I met all the big shots of the time. I got married in 1928, and at the same time, they started to have a problem in the radio industry. They were selling radio sets in Oshkosh and every other little town, and in those places a person who had a radio would go to a local guy for repairs and the guy didn't know what he was doing. He had to write to New York to the manufacturers for the circuits. There was a book that was kept at the time of various radios because each circuit was different and each color code was different. So the radio industry decided that they had to have a standard system. And I was appointed to represent the public with the engineers to devise a color code that would be standard for the United States. The color code means there's a resistor in there; they color the resistors with three types of colors so the guy knows the blue is a thousand, green is five hundred, and yellow is two—so that's the worth of those resistors in ohms. They still use that same color code all over the world. The only thing different in the world today is that the plug is different in Europe. The electric people never got together to produce a standard plug. Those were the days when Steinmetz was the chief engineer in New York City, and he devised alternating current against Edison's direct current because he said that if you put a transformer up you can feed many houses, while with direct current you got to feed from the powerhouse directly to each house. And that was uneconomical. I had worked in Germany on fluorescent lights and also transmission of power, so I was interested in this area. Then I formed my own company that made amplifiers. That was Radio Laboratories. I was associated with the International Ladies Garment Workers Union. Father was a friend of David Dubinsky's. They needed amplifiers for their dining room. I built the most elaborate dining room amplifier—they used it from 1927 or 1930 until a couple of years ago. The reason I got into amplifiers was not only for that one. I built one for Franklin Roosevelt, who was sponsored by the ILGWU, and they needed amplifiers on their trucks for him and we had to design an amplifier where he could sit on his chair and we could amplify his voice. At that time there was terrible equipment because no good theory was being used in their construction. After a while we even kicked out Madison Square Garden's amplifier and put our own in. Bootleggers used to come to Radio Labs and asked for radios so they could pinpoint two stations to find the middle point. If you land booze, you have to know where you're landing. And I built that kind of equipment for them. Every time I built that kind of equipment, it was with the logical theory that I had learned to use when I was in school in Germany. Then I wrote two articles—one appeared in the *New York Sun* and one in *Radio Engineering* in 1931. While I was with Radio Laboratories, we dealt with the problem of theater audiences that couldn't hear what was going on. It was this new wave in the theater of talking natural talk instead of projecting. We had to devise microphones that weren't obvious. They had to have enough pickup, no reverberations so that the loudspeakers wouldn't feed back but also be loud enough for the audience to understand what goes on in the theater. The experimenting was all done in burlesque houses, because in legitimate theaters we had to have a union man stand by for every man that was there. If you brought three people, you had to have three union people there as well, so immediately the cost of the operation was silly. But the burlesque houses were not unionized, so we could spend hours experimenting. We developed microphones with air between two plates that are tight and would change with the velocity of voice vibrations, so we had a much clearer and much brighter sound than they got with the ribbon mikes that were being used at the time. So we designed this kind of microphone, and everybody was interested. I was impressed by the work of a man named Nikola Tesla that everybody thought was nuts, like Steinmetz, because he proposed that you could transmit power without line but by air. Everybody insisted that you couldn't broadcast power without line. But he devised the theory for it, and it's still used today—it's one of the reasons that we're able to do a lot of things in space. He died a broken-hearted man, but he wrote a book about his theory which is standard today. His publisher came to me and said, "Why don't you write a book about your theories and about how we can apply this to everyday use by repairmen and engineers?" So I put together a book and showed examples that only two things can happen in electronics—either you have an open or a short. Nothing else can happen, and I gave simple tests with a battery and a meter and a lamp to find out where the short is or to show if it's open. Since you had a color code to work with, when you found the part that was open or the part that was short, you could replace what needed repair because you knew its value. So I went back to my association and worked with the standards committee and applied my theories. The manual that I put together was used by the Marine Corps during World War II and also by Army organizations in the field. That period of my activity ended in 1935 when I moved to 117 West 46th Street, where I built the equipment for radio station WEVD.[8] Because I had built their equipment, they asked me to do recording for them, too, and then I got involved in the record business and met Leadbelly. He really put me in the record business, because I got national publicity through my association with him.

**B:** I've always wondered if the name of your record company came from William Graham Sumner's book, *Folkways.*

**A:** The name did come from the famous book by Sumner [published in 1907]. The idea came to me from George Herzog, who was a colleague of Harold Courlander, my first editor in the Ethnic series. Herzog was a professor emeritus at Columbia. He said Rich von Hornbostel had collected a lot of ethnic music in Germany and he had many of those things. They had lost a lot through our bombardings of the libraries in Berlin where they were housed. They were mostly on wax cylinders, which are very breakable. So all the early collections of the people's material is lost. And he said that he would like me to start this series of ethnic materials for him. He and Courlander worked on that. Courlander had just come back from Haiti and Cuba, and he gave me the recordings to publish. Through Herzog I also met Willard Rhodes, who was interested in musical anthropology—in those days the term ethnomusicology hadn't been invented yet. Rhodes had a collection of American Indian materials that he wanted me to issue, and I said I'd love to. I wanted there to be a written documentation as well, so I issued a booklet along with the record, and that became my first Ethnic album—number 4401 [*Music of the Sioux and Navajo*]. Then I started to get a lot of offers of material that I didn't know anything about, so I paid Courlander a little every week. I said this is too important, someone who knows this field ought to be in charge. Now I know a lot more about it, but then I was scared of it. The general folk materials I could handle myself, but it took more specialized people for other things. It was Herzog's idea to use the word *ethnic* for the tribal recordings and others similar to that.

**B:** That was a time when the idea of documentation was very much in the air.

**A:** My brother Nathan was involved with the Federal Writer's Project. He also worked on a film project and he also went to the South. Ben Shahn was in that film project, too, and there were many photographers doing documentation. The young writers couldn't earn a living, and Shahn and other painters couldn't make a living either; but he was a terrific photographer. In those projects Nathan did the written documentation. They were doing the books of the states, and there was the Rivers of America series. Each publisher did a different state. Nathan was involved also in motion pictures, and since I was an electronic guy, he called me in, and I did the lighting for the films—of course, I didn't get paid for that. The Depression was a time when people were looking back to find out what was happening to them, and the idea of preserving the memories was important. Right from the beginning I let my literary background become part of the work. That was the difference with Folkways recordings—every album had extensive notes and documentation of the singers and the cultures. Father forbade the children to become writers—he thought it would take money away from him. Nathan was the only one that told him to go to hell and became an author anyway. I was never good at that myself, but in this way I could create a book rather than writing it. What I had put together was a talking book, and that's what got people interested. The first album I ever issued was Father's *In the Beginning,* children's stories of the Bible which he interpreted. I had the publisher give me some material that I could use for documentation of the three-record set. And that established the pattern for everything I did. I had been thinking that way for so long it wasn't intellectual, it was just a natural reaction. After several starts and a bankruptcy, Folkways Records began in 1948.

**B:** How did the connection with Leadbelly come about?

**A:** Those were the first independent records that I did, with Huddie Ledbetter, Leadbelly. Leadbelly came to me through filmmaker Sy Rady. He was an independent producer of plays and shows on Broadway when he was very young. And he was associated with ILGWU. He put on *Pins and Needles.* That was the first musical on Broadway that took such a social approach. Until then it was straight musicals or plays by Eugene O'Neill. Sy got backing from ILGWU and did *Pins and Needles.* I was there because of my earlier association with the ILGWU and what I could do about sound. And there I met Sy, and he was interested in what I was doing. John Lomax—I hated his guts, but he was a terrific guy—he had just produced the March of Time movie about Leadbelly. He dressed him up as a convict, and he would drag him around to show what a great guy John Lomax was because he was his guardian. And he had helped to get him out of jail and recorded Leadbelly for the Library of Congress. I guess by that time Leadbelly had been singing for progressive and left groups. So Sy brought Leadbelly around, and immediately Leadbelly and I were brothers. I understood him, he understood me, and he utilized me; and I was willing to be used because he knew that through me and through my medium he was able to express what he wanted. He was a great intellect. A real, hard-thinking, practical man. He was not like Josh White and other guys who sang just to make money. He really understood what he was, in terms of America, in terms of music and everything else. Fred Ramsey, a documenter and photographer, was very friendly with Leadbelly, and they lived together for a while. Fred was a bachelor, and Leadbelly needed a place to stay. Fred did recordings in a more informal setting than the studio, and in those sessions they just sat around and ate and drank and then Leadbelly picked up his guitar and started to sing and tell about his life. And I issued all those.[9]

**B:** I'd like to hear about your famous studio.

**A:** My studio at that time at 117 West 46th Street was very open. Marian Distler, my assistant, did the books, and I had the equipment. Actually, the recording equipment that I built and used in those early days is still being used by a recording studio in New York—that's almost fifty years. There was a window, and my equipment was against it. Marian was close with a desk and files. And on the other end was a studio that I insulated and built, about fifteen by ten feet. The door was on the other side and you walked into the studio. That was the famous studio where so much work was done. So we were always in the place, either Marian or me, and other people used to come in and say, "I want to record," so all I had to do was get off the desk and put the equipment on and record. Nobody ever had to call beforehand to make appointments, because they all knew I was there twelve to fourteen hours a day. It was no problem to record them. I had already done those earlier recordings and sound work in burlesque houses and with the Bagelman sisters [they became the Barry Sisters] and Einstein. I always believed in the "one mike" theory—I never accepted the idea of several mikes and mixing. This is the way the mike sounds, and this is the way I hear it. So I only had the one mike on a stand. I even recorded major concerts in Carnegie Hall with one mike. Of course, it had to be set in the right place. The mikes we used had this beautiful natural quality. And that's still my theory—I hate the stereo recordings, and mixing can never give you the accurate sense of the original sound. That's what I wanted to preserve and document, the actual sound that was there. So I always started to record flat, never with a peak on it, because you were never able then to reconstruct the way it was. Let the equipment have the peaks as you're listening. A hundred years from now it is as natural as the day I recorded it. And that approach also comes from my father. He said to me, "I come across people that are interested in an idea of preserving elements of culture and showing what life is like, and this idea of recording is so unusual that if you develop it you'll have a chance against everybody in the world because you'd be the only one in this business. The others would be fighting with each other for the same things in a commercial way, and you would have a special thing." He told me he had known some collectors, and they were always able to do all right financially. And I translated that into what I was doing. Some of the ones he mentioned were preserving Yiddish books and manuscripts of rare materials that were important. And I had a machine that was able to capture sounds. It was part of my personal background to emphasize natural accuracy and logic and intellectual concerns. Nothing comes just from the air. It all comes from deep thinking about what's important in life—and then to find a technical way of saving that.

**B:** Your relationship with Pete Seeger is another thing that interests me very much.

**A:** I made more than fifty records with Pete Seeger and I still find him a very hard man to understand. Only Pete knows Pete. I don't even think Toshi [his wife] knows Pete, and she is closest to him. Pete has a very interesting and very unusual background. He comes from an old American-German family, bankers, who kicked his father, Charlie, out of the house because he became a musicologist and not a banker. He was one of the greatest musicologists who ever lived, one of the people who invented the idea of ethnomusicology. So Charlie became a well-known musicologist, and the government put him in charge of some programs in connection with the Pan-American Union. And Pete was never comfortable in those circumstances. His father was a gentleman, always well-dressed and looking proper and behaved in a genteel way. And Pete must have had a very rough time. First, he had a mother who was very eccentric but a good musician; and then he had a stepmother, Ruth Crawford Seeger, a great musicologist and composer, one of the first important documenters. And I think he couldn't figure out where he fit in the midst of all that. So he broke away and tried to find himself in the course of his involvement with folk music, as if there he might find his roots. He never discussed this with me—this is my own speculation, but I think it's right. He took off on a long trip around the country. On the bum. That was the hippie trip of the period; that's what you did—you went on the road and lived off the people and you said to hell with society. And it seems to me that was the basis for the logic of his life. He learned how to pick a banjo and how to make music. He also learned how to behave in society, to become more social. So by the time he came to me, he was already formed in this way. And we had the strangest talks when we first met. The way we met was like this: there was a session at Decca about Lincoln, *The Lonesome Train*.[10] I got a phone call from Alan Lomax, who said, "Stay in your studio because Pete Seeger is in town, and we're coming to record." He said Pete had to go back to army camp in New Jersey, and then he may go overseas. So I stayed in the studio. They got through at Decca about four in the morning, and Pete had to be back in camp about nine that same morning. So from the studio where they did the record for Decca, he came to me. And we were introduced, and he did the first album we did together, 2003—I forget the name. [It was a ten-inch LP, *Darling Corey.*] That's how I met Pete. During that time we started work on the Lincoln Brigade album and a lot of other things. I would start a discussion about something that would interest me, and Pete would change the subject and try to convince me to do something that he was interested in. So I could never ask him, "Where are you going? What are you doing?" He always wanted to do what he wanted, immediately, right at the moment. And I had to pay attention to what he wanted to do. And as a result he created my whole folk music concept. Because he created ideas and songs and every time he had an idea I went along with it—and there are those fifty albums that we did. Every one is Pete's idea. I tried to work with all my artists that way—I wanted to know what they had to say and how they wanted to say it. That's what it meant to me to be a documenter.

**B:** Did you work that way with Woody Guthrie?

**A:** With Woody it was entirely different. In his own way Woody was the most anti-social person I ever met. He didn't like people, especially middle class, bourgeois people. When he came to New York, he didn't meet people of his own kind, his own background. But he had a driving force and a knowledge of what he stood for. He felt that he represented a group of poor people that needed to be spoken for, and he wanted to give them exposure. When you talked to Woody he behaved like a hippie—that's the closest word. He would sit on the floor, he'd look in one direction and say a couple of words, that's all; then he'd go home and write me a beautiful, long letter, more lucid than his talking. He was a terrific writer. As long as I didn't bother him and contradict him but listened to him and used his idea, he felt comfortable with me. Woody would create a song right there in the studio. When Woody got in front of a microphone, he knew exactly what the guitar was going to sound like and what he was going to sound like. He was using me like a pen, to make a book. I was working the machinery, but he was using it for himself. I never looked at his hair, his way of dressing. That was Woody, you accepted Woody the way he was. He had just walked into the studio one day, sat down on the floor and said, "I'm Woody Guthrie." I said, "So what?" Later on we became good friends. I helped him in the sense that as soon as he wrote down the song, he would rush to the studio to record. We were always ready for him. He would try the song immediately with the tune that he had in his head. He always used a folk tune for the words he wrote. He'd make two or three versions of the thing until the tune sounded right to him. He could say, "I like this song, I don't like this song, and put this album out." Then I would suggest that he do something about Sacco and Vanzetti, to go to Boston and see the places where it actually happened and interpret it in a ballad form. He took Cisco Houston with him and he did it. And he appreciated that what I had to say had a validity, and I treated him like a human being who had something important to say. But generally you would think he was the strangest person in the world.

**B:** I know you think of yourself as an editor. How much input do you need in a production?

**A:** I feel that if I put a man on record, that man must know what he's trying to say. So there's no reason for me to provide guidance. And so I generally give artists and collectors complete freedom to do their work as they want to. The only area I feel strongly about in terms of editorial supervision and I'm pretty strict about it, is in the children's field. Many people who write children's materials treat them like babies. I have now in front of me by a young author the most terrific story about dinosaurs—why the big ones died and the little ones survived. I have a six-year-old grandson who lives in Canada (my son Michael is an anthropologist there), and once when I took him to the Museum of Natural History, he read off the names of those damn dinosaurs when I couldn't get to the third letter. And this author writes for kids as if they couldn't understand a new idea. And yet you can see how much they are ready for. So even though the concept is wonderful, the language and the way the ideas are presented are not acceptable. So I talk to the author and try to get him to relate to the children in an interesting and mature way. I do that with every one of the people who send me children's materials. I am careful to see that the words can be understood by children and that the approach doesn't treat them as if they can't understand important ideas and issues. I'm very strict about that, and it has made a lot of difference in the quality. Over half our sales come from children's albums. I just won't allow anybody to talk down to children.

**B:** Is there a secret to the remarkable success of your Folkways operation?

**A:** I have almost 1,800 albums in my catalogue now; I keep every one of them in print by using the kind of logic that I learned in Germany in my early days. A lot of people come to me to find out how I do this—people like Rounder, Flying Fish, and others—but I'm not sure they figure it out. Right now this is a big business, but there are only three people working here. I learned in Germany how to handle the business in a logical fashion. It's like the logic that one and one is two, and if you follow that through from the recording to the finished album, you have it made.

**B:** Do you have any notions of retiring?

**A:** No way. I'll die in the traces. But I have made an arrangement that the whole catalogue will go to the Smithsonian Institution and they will carry on the work.[11]

# Appendix Two
# Buell Kazee:
# An Interview and
# Banjo Instructor

When I rediscovered Buell Kazee in the summer of 1957 he was serving as the pastor of a Baptist church in Lexington, Kentucky. At that time most folklorists knew of his impressive recordings released by Brunswick records between 1927 and 1929 and assumed, as I did, that he was long dead. The fifty-two sides (published just before the Great Depression put Brunswick out of business) became the classic examples of authentic Kentucky singing and banjo-picking. But it was not only the economic slump that kept Kazee from pursuing his musical career along commercial lines. His religious commitment led him to turn down the offers to appear in vaudeville and other show-biz environments. Consequently, even in his native state only the early recordings continued to give testimony to his legendary reputation. Kazee was a highly educated man whose traditional talents were not diminished by his commercial ventures in the twenties, but he was not exceptional in his ability to meld folk and popular styles of expression.

When I met him, Kazee was anxious to do a taped interview in which he could talk about his life and record his vocal and instrumental virtuosity. The ensuing Folkways album was among the first in which a folk artist had an opportunity to talk as well as play;[1] I had been very much influenced by the classic interviews of jazz great Jelly Roll Morton that Alan Lomax did for the Library of Congress. Kazee, who died in 1976, was basically a gentle and modest man who understood quite well that there was no great market for his kind of music. But the record brought him to the public's attention again and provided opportunities for him to perform at schools and festivals around the country. Although he enjoyed his visits with me at California State University, Fresno (where he and his wife were my house guests), he was often upset by later meetings with counter-culture folkies at various festivals. When he heard the many protest songs that were in vogue then, Kazee would often sing his brilliant version of "The Orphan Girl," in which the little girl freezes to death while the rich man "slept on his velvet couch." He would insist, "That's a real protest song."

Twenty years later, when some Kentucky folklorists decided to release a recording of Kazee's subsequent work, he complained bitterly about the entire occasion of our recording session and its aftermath. Loyal Jones, who did the notes, printed all of Kazee's comments without checking any of them with me.[2] It was partly sour grapes on Jones's part; I had shown an interest in Kazee long before anyone in Kentucky had. Like many old-time musicians, Kazee was frustrated by the fact that country and pop singers cashed in mightily on their versions of traditional materials, while those who had provided the sources could only impress a small crowd of mostly northern revivalists. In the 1920s Kazee had received a flat fee for his work and no opportunity for royalties—even if there had been any. But according to Jones, it was not the earlier disappointments but my mistreatment of Kazee that prevented him from making any more recordings.

As a matter of fact, in addition to the Kazee material, I had collected a great deal from other performers whose work was of great interest to Folkways and some of the other small companies that specialized in publishing traditional materials. I saw very clearly the problems that I and other collectors were facing from a system that inevitably left the artists unhappy while editors often had to offend the sensitivities of their clients in order to bring the materials to light for a small audience. When Moe Asch produced an album of my own performances of songs I had collected in Minnesota, I was astounded to see that all had been copyrighted.[3] When I complained to Asch he explained that he was in danger of being sued by groups that took public domain material from his records, copyrighted them, and then sued Folkways! Charles Seeger had suggested a system where the Library of Congress handled such materials, apportioning the royalties equally among the artists, collectors, and companies. But no one attempted to implement his idea.

Although Kazee remained on friendly terms with me, he sent Asch some viciously insulting letters, claiming that there were significant amounts of money due him. Asch and many of his editors weathered these assaults throughout their careers. I decided not to, even if it meant not releasing some valuable materials. One album would have contained the repertoire of a fabulous performer of folk hymns and mining songs. Asch had already accepted it for publication when I told him not to proceed.

That is why I waited so long to release the materials that follow. I had encouraged Kazee to publish comparable materials on his own, but, while he seemed interested, he never developed the projects. The banjo instructor and an accompanying record would have been especially useful. The interview was done in 1958, the same time as the one that appears on the Folkways recording of Kazee's work. It provides some important insights into the early history of recordings of traditional materials and suggests some corrections for our ideas about their basic characteristics.

Kazee was highly literate and fully trained in college as a musician, yet he was still capable of reproducing the folk styles he learned when he was growing up. Like a great many other American performers, Kazee was competent in more than one style and could easily switch from folk style to his concert voice and maintain each with full integrity. His description of his encounter with the New York recording specialists makes it clear that they knew very well what they were looking for. They were careful to prevent him from using what he called his "good voice" (the concert voice) when he made the recordings. Among other things it meant avoiding vibrato and sticking to his Kentucky dialect in pronunciation.

Kazee was always interested in developing his own compositions based on folk materials and directed toward popular and light classical audiences. Like many traditional performers, he underestimated the value of his folk repertoire, remarking to me on many occasions that one classical piece was worth more to him than all his traditional tunes. But he was also very careful about preserving his materials. His New York producers kept him mainly to his traditional repertoire, though he did a few pop numbers as well. This mixed mode is more the rule than the exception among many of the best performers in the United States; they have been proficient in pop, jazz, and, like Kazee, sometimes in semi-classical or concert traditions as well. American folk style was, after all, thoroughly mixed with English and European popular traditions as well as eighteenth- and nineteenth-century American popular music elements, the sources of poplore.

Kazee's formal musical training is a key factor in his banjo style and his ability to describe it. I had suggested that there would be a good deal of interest in a banjo method based on his impressive approach to the instrument. In February 1959 he sent the description that is reproduced here with this comment:

The matters enclosed are crude. I rushed through the best I could, but I found it difficult to write. You know enough about this to fix it in an order that will best serve your purposes. I have gone a little farther and have given some indication of how the instrument is played. I could with care, work out a pretty reliable method, with some illustration of the strings, but thought you might get this with a little work. Certainly it should be illustrated and perhaps demonstrated before any one could read it. I would choose better symbols, etc.

I have corrected a few obvious errors in his tablature, but the method is otherwise as he sent it and indicates very well the unique aspects of his style. Although he shows the thumb on the fifth string (like most Kentucky "frailers"), he actually moved his thumb down to the first and second strings, sometimes even stroking back up with his thumb to achieve his "rollicking effect." By dropping his thumb and "double-noting" Kazee developed a style close to what we now call "clawhammer"; he was able not only to play melody along with the fiddlers but also to work out intricate patterns in racing rhythms under his vocals. Among my favorites is a motif of sixteenth-notes, which he achieved by dropping his thumb and pulling off on the first string. It is especially effective in modal tunings.

Kazee's emphasis on a loose and relaxed position of the right hand is also characteristic of his special approach. Most banjo frailers keep the hand and fingers quite stiff. (Mandolin virtuoso Kenny Hall maintains that farmers developed frailing because their hands were so cramped from the exertions of farm work.) Kazee used to complain about players who "throw their hands"—in a stiff position it is necessary to do so. Because he could pick the melody and develop effective patterns to support his singing, he needed a more flexible and loose technique. He also liked to play close to the fingerboard and away from the bridge, which gave a sweeter, less strident sound than banjos ordinarily produce.

No one has yet defined fully the significance of the many open tunings traditional banjo players used. Ultimately the technique was transferred to the guitar by the early blues "bottleneck" style virtuosos such as Robert Johnson and others. Kazee has noted that "the object is to get as many open strings as possible" to facilitate noting and in his case to pick out the actual melodies. Fiddlers use open tunings for the same reason. I have heard theories that Paganini often cheated by using open tunings rather than the standard one for his complicated compositions; some contemporary performers of Paganini's work have been accused of the same thing. Kazee explained that every song is associated with a particular tuning, though there are some that he uses for only one specific song.

Aside from his skill as a traditional performer, Kazee's ability to express himself in more than one style exemplifies the poplore genre. I have never heard a banjo picker who didn't play marches and know a good many pop or jazz tunes. But because collectors usually get what they are looking for, folklorists have often missed the implications of this mixing of styles, screening out materials that do not fit their preconceptions. This oversight is damaging in a multicultural society such as ours where not only styles but levels of culture have been consistently syncretized. The established view has shown us folk artists untainted by other levels of culture, but close examination reveals a very different picture, of materials working together to form American folk styles.

There is irony in the fact that if the biographical information about Kazee had been known when he was recorded, he might have been characterized as a "revival" musician, if not associated with fakelore. If we continue to pay more attention to the full context of American folk tradition (and especially to the ethnic traditions that flourish here), new models of the folk process will have to be developed that reflect more accurately what these documents reveal about a multifaceted sensibility such as Buell Kazee's, not about a pure, isolated, and undifferentiated folk mind that has no basis in actual experience.

## The Interview

(Kazee has just finished singing "The Swapping Song.")

**Kazee:** He swaps and swaps and swaps, which makes it look like a play-party song. It goes on to rats and mice, you know, and all that. I remember mother singing that. One of the first songs I ever heard and she didn't know it all, but she didn't know it was a play-party song either and I didn't either. We all just accepted it, you know. The word tare—"Then I rode from t-a-r-e to tare"—was probably an old English word for town, and it's quite old. It's Elizabethan by all means. I guess if we knew the game, why they would take one or the other, probably one of them's named mule and one of them's named cow.

**Bluestein:** Every time you swapped you changed.

**K:** Yes, that's right. Well, many little snatches and fragments of songs we'd hear never meant anything except as something to sing, and lots of times they'd seem to be made up on the spur of the moment. But these vagrant stanzas that you'd hear going all around would fit any kind of song. I remember hearing Taylor Connaly when he'd come across the field, coming down to his house just above our house on the creek. He'd sing, "Who'll pick the banjer? / Who'll sing the song? / Who'll court them pretty girls, / When I'm dead and gone?" Then as a sort of refrain he'd end up by singing, "Oh, My Rhodie gal, trouble on my mind." Well, that's a "Lonesome Road" idiom there, almost. You can feel it. And Rhodie must have been his girl. Whatever girl it was, he'd sing. And then I can think (when I take time to think) of half a dozen of those little things. Now, when a dance was held at our house—a bean cutting, bean hulling, or bean stringing, or an apple cutting or something like that—they'd do the work first and gather round, you see, and push the beds back against the wall and have a dance, and that was the young people's get-together. Well, as they would come riding their mules up the creek or riding down the road across the hill, you'd hear them singing little snatches of songs like that, you know. Some of them maybe singing long, lonesome songs or several stanzas of them. But I can go back to memory now, when just as darkness settled down and the Saturday evening crowd was to gather, I'd hear those echoes of people coming in all directions and hear their songs. I can think of those little snatches that don't mean anything at all.

**B:** What were they. Can you think of any you can sing?

**K:** Well, right off I can't. Some would sing, "Shady Grove," you know— "Shady Grove my little love, / Shady Grove I'm bound, / Shady Grove my little love, / I'll meet you when the sun goes down." And then they'd sing, "If I had a needle and thread, / Fine as I could sew, / Sew my true love to my side, / And down the river I'd go." Well, that happened to be one that came to my mind, but I can't think of any others right now. But that was typical.

**B:** I want to talk a little bit about some traditional forms of singing, and I'm wondering how you would distinguish between hillbilly and folk.

**K:** Well, what is commonly called hillbilly did derive from the mountains as distinguished from the outlanders and it's not an old term—it came into use during the last half century. And people thought of hillbillies as being somebody raised back in the hills who had the customs and songs and so forth. But what is now called hillbilly is modern, commercialized tunes somewhat in the style of the old folk tunes. The genuine article is not known today on radio. They write those things. They're close in that they are simple and folksy in a way, but the tunes are all about the same. They're bagpipe range. It's just about the same old thing except its commercialized and put in a rhythmic form so that it can be very popular. They moved the hillbilly up some and brought the other folk down some and put them in the middle and made a great commercial thing out of it. And that's exactly what happened to a lot of this Stamps Baxter music and that stuff you hear in the sacred line.

**B:** These are the people who are writing new stuff.

**K:** Yeah, but they write it in the old style somewhat. It's not as folksy as the old mountain ballads were; they were too far back to get the rhythm and action and the excitement that they have in the modern hillbilly stuff. Modern hillbilly stuff is commercialized stuff. It's just produced for that business, you see. And it's to reach that vast audience of people who don't want to go into the classics and semi-classics. Naturally, there are more of those than there are of anybody else. A lot of it is rowdy and characteristic of the spirit of the young people who turn loose and go to town. They're not isolated any more.

**B:** This is true of even the instrumental styles.

**K:** Yes, sir. Why the first real old music that we had—take the guitar, for instance—this is not a mountain instrument at all. It's an imported thing. Nobody ever played a guitar when I was a boy in our country. But when a man came through with a traveling picture show when I was a little boy about ten or twelve years old, he had a guitar player. The first one we ever heard of in the style that he played, and he played and sang to furnish the music for that fast moving-picture show in those old days. He went to school houses and so forth. That guitar was the talk of the country, but it wasn't characteristic. The dulcimer—that old, long, coffin-shaped instrument which is not really a dulcimer, but it's called that—that was a three-stringed instrument. That was a characteristic instrument and Jean Ritchie plays that some. But the banjo and the fiddle, those are true Appalachian instruments. You'd go down to the courthouse and they'd be sawing a fiddle and singing a lonesome tune or playing a banjo. And they'd play the banjo and fiddle together in dances—they make a fine combination.

**B:** But when you hear a lot of—even the instrumentalists sound like hillbillies. The kind of complexity, for example, that I hear when you play your banjo is a kind of rhythmic and melodic complexity. It's very noticeably absent in most of the hillbilly songs. It's just playing on a couple of chords over and over again.

**K:** Well, you see, this slide guitar that they brought in was originally known in this country as the Hawaiian guitar.

**B:** Steel guitar, I think they called it.

**K:** Yes, they call it steel guitar now; we called it Hawaiian guitar and on the old phonographs we had some records of the Hawaiian guitars and they were the true instruments. They were played by Hawaiians. But later, everybody came to—well, it's just a late thing somewhat—steel guitar is. Then when it got this magnified tone—what do you call it?

**B:** Amplified.

**K:** Amplified tone. Then everybody went crazy about the steel guitar. Of course, it had great possibilities. But they've taken the fiddle, they've added to the fiddle—you don't hear many banjos played in a characteristic style on the radio. Very few of them play like I do. There's a woman out Midwest playing and two or three others that play that way. But if they play a banjo, it's done in a more modern style and they combine a banjo and a fiddle and, of course, they call it a fiddle but they really do a lot of violin stuff on it and add to that the big bull fiddle and maybe an accordion and a steel guitar and so on, and that's a rollicking modern band as far as that's concerned, you see. That's what they call hillbilly stuff today. But that's not characteristic folk hillbilly at all. So I would distinguish hillbilly as a modern version of folk music and a highly commercialized version.

**B:** And this is also true of the themes, too.

**K:** Yes.

**B:** Where you have a wide variety of themes—don't you—in the folk music, ranging from ballads to work songs.

**K:** Yes, I would divide them, as I know them, up into the jigs and reels, of course which are the dance tunes—and that's Scotland and Ireland; and then you have the ancient ballads, which are like "Lord Thomas and Fair Elender" and "Barbara Allen" and those that came over. Then you have those that are written in the style of that, like "The Rowan County Crew," which is a story of a feud here in Rowan County, or "The Ashland Tragedy." Those are the only two broadsides I ever saw.

**B:** By that you mean songs written about an actual occurrence?

**K:** Yes, actual occurrence. The Tollivers and Martins up there in Rowan County. I lived there for twenty-two years right close to where this place was. Jean Thomas has that in her book and she tells a lot about that Rowan County feud and all that. And then several other tunes like that are written in the style of the ballads, most of them tragic. And, of course, you have the love songs, love ballads; then you have the heroic ballads, I'd say like "Big John Henry" and "John Hardy" and those. And then you have the moon-shine ballads, which are all very definitely Eastern, characteristic of our mountain country and all that. Those work songs are close to the—I'd say— heroic ballads, and that gets the major classification.

**B:** Of course, you would have a whole area of children's songs, too.

**K:** Yes, the play-party songs. Of course, sacred songs. They are not associated as hillbilly or folk music so much until recently. I have been interested in developing that phase of it. And these old songs that the old Baptist brethren—they'd turn over in their graves if they knew that they were love song ballads adapted, you know; the tunes were adapted to their sacred words, but that's what they were. But they were never classified along with these other tunes because religion was a sacred thing and was kept entirely apart from the party songs.

**B:** Yes, and so many people didn't think to look for a connection, but really this was the music the people knew and it would be kind of logical if they would be using it also for their religious tunes as well.

**K:** As a matter of fact, some of those love ballads are just as sad and mournful as some of those religious tunes.

**B:** Especially the death songs, like "That Old Church Yard."

**K:** Yes, that's right. But I don't think much of the word hillbilly any more. I never did object to being called a hillbilly, that's not it. But it's just that it doesn't carry the meaning that it ought to.

**B:** Now when you first went to record, you were telling me about this yesterday and I would like to put it down here because it's a fascinating thing. When was it, 1928?

**K:** Well, no, my first recordings were in 1926. I had picked the banjo since I was five years old and learned slowly and picked at a few dances. But early in life I had joined the church. I was about twelve years old and in those days you couldn't pick the banjo and play the fiddle and belong to the church because the fiddle and banjo had evil associations. And naturally I gave it up for my religion and didn't emphasize it very much. I went on to college—Georgetown College [in Kentucky]—and studied English and majored in English and minored in Greek and Latin and studied music a great deal, and I came to see that we were definitely associated with the Shakespearean world and my music came back. And so I began then to be interested in these songs that I knew and made some collections and played them again on the banjo, and I was beginning teaching voice and preaching along with it there in Ashland, Kentucky; and that's where I ran into a record dealer who had a big store—and records were going like everything then—and he got me to New York immediately and we started making records. That's how I happened to get into it. I made records until 1930 when the crash came and they didn't carry on. I was recording for Brunswick and they dumped their records with Decca, I think, and quit the business. I let them sell out and didn't get all of my records. I made fifty-two selections for Brunswick.

**B:** Now when you first came up there, this was the first time you had ever had the experience of singing into a microphone.

**K:** Oh, yes. You see, they had just begun recording with microphones then. Caruso and all his crowd, they recorded with that tin horn. But they developed the microphone.

**B:** What were your feelings about that when you first sat down in front of it?

**K:** Well, I was scared to death like anybody would be, I reckon. I played some of my most familiar tunes, like "John Hardy," "Rocky Island" and some of those that I could rely on.

**B:** Did it make any difference to you, singing into a microphone, in terms of what you had to do?

**K:** No. It soon became a job. If I had anybody singing with me or playing with me, sometimes it would take three or four recordings to get it. If I did it by myself, why, I would go straight through. No, I soon caught on. I was readily adaptable.

**B:** You said that when you began to sing these songs somebody told you to sing a special way. Who was it?

**K:** Well, see, I had voice training and had been teaching voice and instead of saying "Aw" I would say "I" and all those tones, you know.

**B:** It was diction. They told you to keep it country-sounding.

**K:** Yeah, make it country-sounding and sometimes I'd make it and they'd say, that's fine, but it's too good, it won't sell. They don't want to hear that vibrato in there, and you have to hold your voice down so it doesn't give any evidence of any training. Which was difficult for me to do then. And the words. I remember when I'd sing "Don't forget me little darling" I'd have to say "darling" instead of "darlin'" every time. I couldn't—I just had trained that way, you know and it was very difficult for me to do it. In singing the song, "The Moonshiner,"—"Ah'll go up some dark holler." I'd say "I'll" in spite of everything, instead of saying "Ah'll" like I ought to, you know.

**B:** Who was it that was giving you directions?

**K:** The laboratory manager, Mr. O'Keefe, in New York and Mr. Knapp, he was a Jewish man in Chicago. I went there several times. I remember one time—to show you how important it is—it amazed me to see a little old ditty I'd been singing all my life being talked about in such important terms. You see, Frank Black, a great musician—last I knew of him he was with the International Harvester's orchestra, I believe—you know who he was, don't you? He'd take those little old tunes in there and he'd sit down and arrange them and put so much emphasis on them that I couldn't get the connection. Of course, they were wondering how many times it'd ring in the cash register, you know. That's all they cared about.

**B:** You mean arranging them for orchestration?

**K:** No. Arranging them for the production there on record. Sometimes I'd have Carson Robison. They'd call him in to play the guitar for me, and then they would call Bert Hirsch. I remember a concert violinist and a pianist or two—Bill Wirges played for me some. He's an orchestra director. They'd call those fellows in to give different accompaniments, you see, and sometimes I'd sing by their accompaniments entirely and not by mine. I made quite a variety of records. I made some of Harry von Tilder's old numbers back there in the early days, like "Mandy Lee" and that type of song, you know. He was the Irving Berlin of that time. I don't think he wrote "Mandy Lee" but anyway that type you know. I made different kinds of songs and they tried out all kinds of them. But, of course, I stuck to the folksongs, mainly. I did them exactly like I had done them all my life and never thought about dressing them up like hillbilly stuff is done today, you know. They'd fix it up, but then I gave it the exact recording.

**B:** Well, certainly one thing is that these songs don't need that much dressing up, in that they have enough in themselves.

**K:** But in that day we weren't so commercial. We were not thinking of commercializing so much. Although they were trying to make money out of them, all right, but it wasn't the idea of making a commercial appeal to the kind of trade that you have today.

**B:** Yeah, there was an attitude on their part toward their audience. They were going to give them good stuff and try to make money on it, but still be pretty careful about what they gave them.

**K:** And they thought that the best way to make money was to give it the genuine article, you know. But I think they've decided that maybe lately it was better to—well, taste changes, as you know.

**B:** Taste changes, but you know one thing that's happened within the last, oh, maybe five or six years, is that there must be at least a dozen record labels that are specializing in folk stuff.

**K:** I would like to record some of these old songs I've been singing to these sacred numbers. They need to be pushed a little, and I never have tried to get back into the game. They wanted me to play radio and vaudeville, you know, and stuff like that. And, of course, being a preacher I didn't have any business going into that. Naturally, I backed out. But of course, that's the way to sell records.

## The Banjo Instructor by Buell Kazee

All folk styles of playing a banjo are difficult to explain without demonstration, but we[4] give here the best explanation we can of what is commonly known as the "frailing" style, which we use with adaptations.

The melody is played mainly with the index finger of the right hand. The hand is somewhat relaxed in a fist-like curl with the thumb projecting slightly wide so as to work along the line of the thumb-string. Kazee plays usually just over the end of the fret board where the neck of the banjo joins the head. This allows his arm to rest on the banjo head just back of the highest point in the curve, making the hand drop naturally at that point on the strings. The hand works loosely at the wrist with very slight motion of the arm from there back to the elbow. The curved hand in the right position allows the finger nail of the index finger to be nearly parallel with the strings, the nail pointing back toward the banjo head. The stroke is downward, making the nail hit the string and slide off in a quick, picking stroke just at the forward corner of the nail next to the thumb. (This nail serves as a substitute for a pick.) The thumb works the little short string (fifth string) exclusively. (There are other methods which employ the thumb to pick melody.) The flesh of the index finger may brush the string, and soft playing of the string may be obtained by allowing more of the flesh to brush the string. Conversely, the louder tones are obtained by a more positive and stiff stroke of the nail.

After the beginner has found the idea indicated above, he should now allow the thumb to lie loosely on the neck of the banjo (at the position indicated above) while practicing picking the melody out on the string below. (Note: Don't get in a hurry; Kazee began when he was five and he is now fifty-eight.) As one practices, one will come to see that relaxation of the hand is an art as well as being so necessary. Relaxation is not a slump of the muscles but positive freedom. There is a great difference.

Choosing a melody to learn on is difficult. It should be a tune of very narrow range or one in which progression is easy to follow. We suggest, "Dance Around My Pretty Little Miss" or "Going Down to Town," which is in a different tuning.[5]

### Tuning the Banjo

Of course, for playing the banjo in conventional style there is only one tuning, but for the folk banjo player there are many. In his style of picking, the object is to get as many open strings as possible, thereby eliminating as much fretting as possible (or, as he says, "noting"). Conventional style tuning is, beginning with the long string at the under side of the neck: first string, D above second C (coming down the scale); second string B; third string, G; fourth string C; and the fifth string (or thumb string) G above D of the first string. Now to get more open strings for folk playing, raise the second string to C above middle C (just a step). This brings the succession into this tuning: D, C, G, C, G above second C, the only change being the raise in the second string indicated above. This is one of the two most popular tunings for the banjo, which is, of course, the key of C playing. In the list of tunes played in this tuning are: "Pretty Little Miss," "Soldier's Joy," "Rocky Island," "Moonshiner," "Old Gray Mare," and a long list of "hoedowns" or dance tunes such as, "Chase the Rabbit, Chase the Coon," "Skip to My Lou," "Old Jackie Wilson," "Rock Little Julie," "Baby-O," "Going Down the River," and others. Among the ballads in this tuning are "New Jail" (old Style), "Rowan County Crew," etc.

The other most popular tuning is for "Cripple Creek." (Note: the tuning above was always spoken of as tuning for "Going Down the River," or "Love Somebody"—i.e., "Soldier's Joy.") The fifth string is left in the same position. Lower the second string to the B position of the conventional tuning. Raise the bass or fourth string from C to D. Now you have, beginning with the first string, D, B, G, D, G above second C. This is the key of G major. Many hoedowns and ballads can be played here. Among the hoedowns are: "Cripple Creek," "Down the Line," "Goin' Down to Town," "Cackling Hen," "Shortnin' Bread," etc. Ballads include, "John Hardy," "John Henry," "Wagoner's Lad," "Roll On John," "Little Bessie," etc.

The next easiest tuning from where we are, and most popular for minor tunes is as follows: Simply raise the second string from B to C. This brings the tuning for "Lonesome John," a tune everybody recognized but few could "pick"; but it served as a guide for tuning. In this tuning we can play "The Blind Man," (a ballad composed in America), "The Butcher's Boy," "Old Joe Clark," "Roving Cowboy," "The Girl I Left Behind Me," "East Virginia," etc.[6]

Again: Lower the second string back to B (as in the key of G above); now lower the fifth or thumb string to B immediately above D of the first string. Now you are in tune for "Wild Bill Jones," the only tune I ever played in that tuning.

Again: Put the fifth string back to F above second C; now raise the second string to C (above middle C) and the bass string (fourth) to F above middle C. Now you are in tune for "Shady Grove," and for hoedowns like "Heel Over Head and Toe like a Trigger," "Buck Creek Gals," and maybe others.

Again: Tune in this fashion—D, A, D, G, G above second C. Now you are in tune for "The Yaller Pups." Also the ballad, "The Brown Girl," or "Lord Thomas and Fair Ellender," though sometimes this may be played in another tuning. This is the first tune I learned on the banjo, picking out the melody with the index finger alone. There is another tune to this ballad which is minor (see Brockway-Wyman, *Twenty Kentucky Mountain Songs*) which I consider nearer the original. It is played in the tuning for "Lonesome John."

Again: Tune in this fashion—D, G, F sharp, D, F sharp above second C. Now you are in tune for some "blues" like "Lonesome Road" (as we knew it in the mountains), "Po' Boy, Long Ways from Home." This last is a "bum ballad" with disconnected stanzas depicting a forlorn condition.

Again: Now lower the third string to E and you will have D, G, E, D, F sharp above second C. Here you play "Frankie and Johnnie," "Jay Gould," and a few other snatches of tunes.

Again: Lower the bass string to B below middle C and you have the tuning for "Cumberland Gap." I know of no other tune played in this tuning.

One more, and a very odd tuning, for "Darlin' Corey." Here is a case where you don't need one string, so you just tune it out by making it exactly even with another. The first and second strings are tuned D, D, and the third A, and the fourth D. The fifth is left at F sharp. This is the only tune I know played in this tuning, but I never knew of it being played in any other.

If some of these pitches seem to be too high for singing, as they will be in some cases, we remedied that by simply lowering the strings to a comfortable pitch and keeping the tuning in the same order. In other words, transposing. This totals eleven different ways besides the conventional tuning.

Most of the tunes played in the first open string tuning (for "Love Some-body") I play from conventional tuning. Thus I would not say that all the above is the best way, but it was the way I learned and the usual way among banjo pickers.

### *Playing the Banjo*

If the beginner has now learned the idea of picking out a melody with the finger nail, he may begin to advance to some of the complicated doubling of this finger exercise. Place the finger on the third string and, forgetting about the melody, pick the third string, then the first in succession. If tuned for the key of C [D, C, G, C, G], the succession should be 3–1, 3–1, 3–1, 3–1, 3–1, and so on until you have learned this action. Now wherever the melody leads from one string to another, the first string should be played alternately with the melody note, giving a double action as indicated in the exercise above. In the melody, "Pretty Little Miss," you would have a playing something like this: 1 1 2–1 3 3 4–3 3–2 1 1. (Note: this will not sound right until the proper fretting is done.) Now to make this more intelligible, we will spread it out, and place the fretting beneath each step. The numbers below the string number are the finger and fret.

| 1 | 1 | 2 ——— 1 | 3 | 3 | 4 ——— 3 |
|---|---|---|---|---|---|
| 3–2 | 3–3 | open | 3–2 | 3–2 | open | 3–4 | open |

| 3 ——— 2 | 3 ——— 2 | 1 | 1 |
|---|---|---|---|
| open | open | 3–2 | open | 3–2 | 3–1 |

This includes the first two lines of the melody. Here it is in simple notation (dots show where the melody stays):

Using musical syllables, you have: mi, mi, do, do, la, sol, mi, sol, sol, la, do, mi, mi. Note that in playing this on the banjo, when you come to the first do, we do not repeat the second but revert back to the mi instead to give the doubling effect desired on the banjo. Same with other places where the long dash is indicated.

Now we come to the third stage of the fingering with the right hand. This is a triple stroke, including the two described plus the thumb stroke. Set the middle finger of the left hand on the first string, second fret and hold it there while doing this exercise: Strike the first string with the nail of the index finger as indicated above. Pick the thumb string with the left side of the thumb, letting it brush off the string with a solid but not harsh stroke; then strike the second string with the index finger as above; now the thumb again on the fifth string; now the index finger on the third string, the thumb again, the second string again, and so on. Do this slowly at first, gradually increasing as the technique develops. This should give a rollicking rhythm. In musical notes the progression should be:

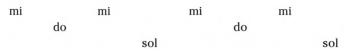

mi               mi               mi              mi
     do                         do
                sol                           sol

Now add another, which we call double-noting. For this, to begin with, just steady the thumb on the edge of the neck in the thumb position. Now with the same fretting as above, stroke downward with the index nail, quickly picking the string with the fretting finger and replacing it before the string is picked again. Musically, coming down the scale, the effect will be:

mi               mi             mi
   re             re           re
     do             do          do     in quick

succession, but the index finger will be making the first and third strokes while the middle tone will be played with the fretting. This can be worked into any series of melody notes and at intervals where time is being marked on longer notes. The reverse exercise is good also, starting on the second string open, picking the first string with the fretting finger, then the stroke on the first string with the fretting finger immediately on the second fret. Then you will have:

         mi             mi           mi
     re           re          re
  do           do          do     and so on.

This will need much practice, but it gives a rippling effect when playing. (Note: Remember, at all times the hand should not be stiff but positive enough to give a solid stroke. Nobody can teach you this; it comes by practice. But when your hand or fingers begin to stiffen, you will know you are headed in the wrong direction. Short, quick strokes are best, and the feeling that the hand is heavy is also best.)

I use another technique for a doubling effect, and for variation, by letting the thumb—after it has picked the thumb string—go down to about the second string and lightly drag back over the second, third, and fourth strings, then picking the thumb string again. This adds still more of the rollicking effect, but like all the rest comes by practice. Like the rest of the hand, the thumb is loose but positive. Then, there is the roll of the right hand. This is executed with the nails of all four right hand fingers dragging backward in immediate succession, making the tips of the nails stroke all four strings. In fact, even though the index finger is making the melody and other notes clear, the other fingers are allowed to brush the strings lightly to give background tines and keep the prominent notes from being so harsh. This is also a partial roll.

There is one other technique with the fretting finger. This is to make one fretting of a string play two notes in succession. Take this melody in the key of C:

This begins on the open third string. The next note is on the second fret of that string. Pick the third string and quickly fret it with the middle finger on the second fret and you will get two notes with one picking. Now you pick the second string open, then pick the first string and quickly fret it on the second fret and you will get a repeat of what you did on the third string. Much of the melodic progression is done this way. When the melody goes up to G—the thumb string—give a roll with the playing hand and pick the thumb string with the thumb once or twice as the rhythm or melody may determine.

# Notes

### Introduction

1. A forceful demonstration of the injustice is in Andrew Hacker, *Two Nations: Black and White, Separate, Hostile, Unequal* (New York: Scribner's, 1992).

2. The pun plays on in August Wilson's *Ma Rainey's Black Bottom,* which has been hugely successful in theaters throughout the country.

3. Jazz musicians, black and white, have often acknowledged the controlling influence of the blues on their work. But popular musicians such as David Bowie make the same point. "In our music, rock 'n' roll, the blues are our mentor, our godfather, everything. We'll never lose that, however modernistic and cliché ridden with synthesizers it becomes. We'll never ever be able to renounce the initial heritage." Quoted in George Lipsitz, *Time Passages: Collective Memory and American Popular Culture* (Minneapolis: University of Minnesota Press, 1990), 103.

4. It is a pity that English lacks so useful a term as the German *volkstümlich.* As in this case, I will usually use the term folk-based as we are not dealing with actual folk styles.

5. See, for example, Houston A. Baker, Jr., *Blues, Ideology, and Afro-American Literature: A Vernacular Theory* (Chicago: University of Chicago Press, 1984); Henry Louis Gates, Jr., *The Signifying Monkey: A Theory of African-American Literary Criticism* (New York: Oxford University Press, 1988); and Arnold Krupat, *The Voice in the Margin: Native American Literature and the Canon* (Berkeley: University of California Press, 1989). Krupat has argued, "To understand better what Native American artists know and think and feel, personally and historically in their material situation; to understand better how a certain traditional commitment to speaking or singing such knowledge and thought and emotion has adapted itself to

writing, may well provoke a rereading, even a reevaluation of other American writers, both older, canonical authors and newer authors on the verge of canonical status. I cannot specify just how such rereading and reevaluating might actually proceed beyond the lines—thematic and technical—already indicated. I would, nonetheless, reaffirm that such rereading and reevaluation must be the consequence of the inclusion of Native American writers (as also Afro-American writers, and women of all groups)" (91). Accenting a different perspective than that of Native Americans results these days in similar calls for revision and inclusion of other marginal voices.

6. Gates, "The Master's Pieces: On Canon Formation and the Afro-American Tradition," in *Conversations: Contemporary Critical Theory and the Teaching of Literature,* ed. Charles Moran and Elizabeth F. Penfield (Urbana: National Council of Teachers of English, 1989), 56.

7. Krupat, *The Voice in the Margin,* 105.

8. Abraham Chapman, ed., *Literature of the American Indians: Views and Interpretations* (New York: New American Library, 1975), 21; Whitman is quoted in Krupat, *The Voice in the Margin.* Krupat has pointed out that the letter (dated 20 July 1883) does not appear in the MLA-approved five-volume edition of Whitman's correspondence.

9. *The Souls of Black Folk* (1903) in *W. E. B. Du Bois: Writings,* ed. Nathan Huggins (New York: Library of America, 1986), 545. It is a tribute to Du Bois's prescience that in his survey of "American music" he included the "music built on Negro themes such as 'Suwanee River,' 'John Brown's Body,' 'Old Black Joe,' etc."

10. The *AHD* suggests that the term comes from a Greek word meaning union, "to unite (in the manner of the Cretan cities) against a common enemy."

11. Archie Green, *Only a Miner: Studies in Recorded Coal-Mining Songs* (Urbana: University of Illinois Press, 1972), 23. Green has maintained that "at the Berkeley Folk Music Festival (June 30, 1967), I suggested *poplore* as a descriptive key-word" (30). The term always has pejorative connotations, in contrast to the "purity" of authentic folklore.

12. John Fiske, *Understanding Popular Culture* (Boston: Unwin, 1989), 15.

13. Andrew Ross, *No Respect: Intellectuals and Popular Culture* (New York: Routledge, 1989), 70.

14. Ibid., 13. One of Ross's countrymen, Ewan MacColl, is in fact a fine example of a poplorist who has taken the "folk-royal culture" of Scotland and turned it into his own effective political expression. A fine singer of traditional ballads, MacColl married Peggy Seeger of the influential Seeger family and created with her a marvelous blend of Anglo-Celtic-American materials.

15. Lipsitz, *Time Passages,* 13.

16. Ibid. 14. As is too often the case with culture studies critics, Lipsitz often undermines his fine perceptions with expressions of oversimplified Marxist class analysis. He concludes a helpful discussion of rock 'n' roll with the following: "The working class in the U.S. exists as an empirical fact in the lives of those trading their labor power for wages, but it also lives in the collective historical memory of the middle class. . . . The working class may not be the agency of emancipation envisioned by Karl Marx, but whatever form emancipation eventually takes, it will be that much easier because there has been an American working class" (132). Marx's more relevant insight has to do with the extent to which the ruling class easily co-opts the poor into striving for the values of the rich. The history of virtually every successful popular musician makes the point clearly.

17. Reebee Garafalo, "Understanding Mega-Events: If We Are the World, Then How Do We change It?" in *Technoculture,* ed. Constance Penley and Andrew Ross, vol. 3 of *Cultural Politics* (Minneapolis: University of Minnesota Press, 1991), 250. For a full discussion of these issues in connection with Guthrie, see Chap. 5.

18. Because folklorists habitually expurgate anything that appears to be popular or commercial (including jazz influences), there develops what appears to be "purely" traditional materials in the work of many old-time singers and instrumentalists. It is just such a tradition that poplorists characteristically react with. As my discussion of Buell Kazee in Appendix 2 reveals, many of those old-timers were already integrated with pop and other commercial sources—if the truth about them were known. Unlike most critics, who use the term pejoratively, W. T. Lhamon explains that "the phase of poplore takes place when an emerging *public* unselfconsciously entertains itself in its inevitably urban environment, so replicates its lore with mechanical (then, later, electronic) means. . . . Like folklore, poplore is nearly always involved with narrative development, with violence, sentimentality, and the excesses of pornography. Unlike folklore, poplore is able to use technical means to ensure slickness, spectacle, and ready accessibility" (*Deliberate Speed: The Origins of a Cultural Style in the American 1950s* [Washington: Smithsonian Institution Press, 1990], 110–11). In his perceptive and wide-ranging study, Lhamon stretches poplore to include too many fields and individuals, but he is right in catching the syncretic elements that poplore revels in.

19. I use the term poplorist to identify artists who take elements from relatively traditional as well as popular sources in creating their characteristic styles. The need for such a term can be seen in the attempts to define the work of performers such as the legendary blues musician, Robert Johnson, who recorded twenty-nine selections in 1936–37 and then

disappeared, rumored to have been murdered by a sweetheart. His songs, according to a recent reviewer, "combine tradition, plagiarism and original creation." Generally described as a "primitive, visionary artist," his vocal and instrumental styles are so overwhelmingly effective that almost every song he recorded has been "covered" by later blues and rock and roll musicians, including The Rolling Stones, Eric Clapton, and Bonnie Raitt. It turns out that far from being primitive "the relentless charge of his delivery was the result of studied arrangement. His tastes and influences were wide-ranging, encompassing not only Delta forebears such as Charley Patton and Skip James, but also Duke Ellington and Bing Crosby." See James Campbell, "The Healing Force of the Blues," *Times Literary Supplement,* 27 July–2 August 1990, 793. "Poplorist" seems to me the appropriate term for such a figure. Johnson's complete recordings are now available on Columbia (records as well as CDs), *Robert Johnson: The King of the Delta Blues Singers.*

20. As Gordon S. Wood points out, "If equality had meant only equality of opportunity or a rough equality of property-holding, it would never have become, as it has, the single most powerful and radical ideological force in all of American history. Equality became so potent for Americans because it came to mean that everyone was really the same as everyone else, not just at birth, not in talent or property or wealth, and not just in some transcendental religious sense of the equality of souls. Ordinary Americans came to believe that no one in a basic down-to-earth and day-in-and-day-out manner is really better than anyone else. That was equality as no other nation has ever quite had it" (*The Radicalism of the American Revolution* [New York: Knopf, 1992], 234). I suggest that the folk ideology I describe derives largely from this part of our history.

21. For a full discussion of literary attempts to infuse American culture with its folk sources, see my study, *The Voice of the Folk: Folklore and American Literary Theory* (Amherst: University of Massachusetts Press, 1972).

22. Charles Seeger, "Folk Music in the Schools of a Highly Industrialized Society," in *Studies in Musicology, 1935–1975* (Berkeley: University of California Press, 1977), 331.

## One  What Is Folk?

1. Modern critics have universally questioned the method and materials of early collectors. For a critique of James G. Frazer, one of the most influential amateur folklorists, see Mary Douglas, *Purity and Danger: An Analysis of the Concepts of Pollution and Taboo* (1966; reprint, London: Ark-Routledge, 1984), Chap. 1.

2. As Stephen Jay Gould has repeatedly emphasized, the authentic Darwinian tradition deals with totally random developments that have absolutely no teleological implications. See his discussion in *Ever Since Darwin* (1980; reprint, New York: Norton, 1982).

3. Here and elsewhere I use the term ideology not in its Marxist sense of false principles but rather to define the underlying arguments upon which notable cultural values rest.

4. Maria Leach and Jerome Fried, eds., *Funk and Wagnalls Standard Dictionary of Folklore, Mythology, and Legend* (1949; reprint, New York: Harper, 1984).

5. Jan Harold Brunvand, *The Study of American Folklore* (New York: Norton, 1968), 4. In fact, not any group will do: certain individuals have been dubbed "revival musicians," meaning that they play folk styles but were born in the wrong place—New York as opposed to Kentucky. Brunvand has also published a collection of what he calls "urban legends," again limited to "White Anglo-American culture" though he explains that the stories "are truly national, often international." A second volume of "new" urban legends resulted from his having become a "celebrity-scholar." Brunvand has noted that "no tale remains static once it enters oral tradition and that modern folklore is extremely fast—aided by the mass media—to reflect current events." See *The Vanishing Hitchhiker* (New York: Norton, 1981).

6. Because Native Americans are generally considered in the framework of tribal societies, they fit well under the folk rubric. But in fact, most folklorists leave the discussion of Native American culture to ethnomusicologists.

7. Tristram Potter Coffin and Hennig Cohen, eds., *Folklore from the Working Folk of America* (New York: Anchor-Doubleday, 1974), 27.

8. One always needs to be wary about Old World-New World juxtapositions because they are often based on a complete dismissal of the Native American culture which was extant when populations from the Old World arrived. The New World was not literally a *tabula rasa* waiting for European imprints.

9. Quoted by Richard Middleton in the introduction to *Popular Music* (Cambridge: Cambridge University Press, 1981), 1:3–4.

10. Alex Haley, *Roots* (New York: Doubleday, 1976). No one could have predicted the phenomenal success of the television series based on the book, which dealt with the idea of roots for blacks. (Americans of Slavic origin talk about "rootskies," the Irish of tubers.) But all Americans, regardless of their cultural background, seemed fascinated by the question of their origins, lost in the immigrations to the New World. The roots phenomenon provides many insights into the nature of the American experi-

ence and relates directly to the emergence in the 1990s of a virulent attack on multiculturalism by rightwingers who claim it undermines the integrity of our culture.

11. Jeff Todd Titon, *Downhome Blues Lyrics: An Anthology from the Post-World War II Era,* 2d ed. (Urbana: University of Illinois Press, 1990), 3.

12. Richard M. Dorson, ed., *Folklore and Folklife: An Introduction* (Chicago: University of Chicago Press, 1972), 2–5.

13. Henry Glassie, *The Spirit of Folk Art: The Girard Collection at the Museum of International Folk Art* (New York: Abrams, 1989), 31.

14. William A. Wilson, "1990 Archer Taylor Memorial Lecture," *Western Folklore* 50 (1991): 129.

15. Robert A. Georges, "Earning, Appropriating, Concealing, and Denying the Identity of Folklorist," *Western Folklore* 50 (1991): 11–12.

16. Elliot Oring, "On the Future of American Folklore Studies: A Response," *Western Folklore* 50 (1991): 75.

17. Alan Dundes, *The Study of Folklore* (Englewood Cliffs, N.J.: Prentice-Hall, 1965), 2.

18. In a more recent essay, Dundes has argued that folklore expresses the various aspects of a group's identity. "The idea that folklore can express a group's identity is not a new one," he has written. "Indeed, it was Herder who claimed centuries ago that the soul of a people was expressed in that people's folk-songs." Dundes's note refers to Robert Ergang's important work as well as the biography by Robert T. Clark, Jr. "Defining Identity through Folklore," in *Folklore Matters* (Knoxville: University of Tennessee Press, 1989), 9. Refreshingly, he does not use the epithet "romantic nationalism" in reference to Herder's views.

19. Brunvand has published six volumes of what he calls "American folk narratives" or urban legends. They consist of tales told as true but exhibiting all the marks of traditional tales. Brunvand seems surprised that these exist since "they are an integral part of White Anglo-American culture and are told and believed by some of the most sophisticated 'folk' of modern society—young people, urbanites, and the well educated." Stuck with the conventional criteria for folklore, Brunvand still highlights white culture (as if blacks don't have similar traditions) and accepts the assumption that urban, educated people are incapable of folk creativity. Yet his books provide the evidence that they do; it doesn't, however, lead him to question the premises of his mentors. The sixth of Brunvand's volumes is entitled *The Baby Train and Other Lusty Urban Legends.* It tells us little about the significance of these materials, now simply urban legends rather than "new" urban legends. The title suggests erotica, but as usual the materials are thoroughly bowdlerized. Brunvand explains that they were first published in his Utah family newspaper columns. As a reviewer noted, "Brun-

vand is doing an excellent job of recording for us these urban legends. What we need next is someone to analyze them to find out what they are saying" (Rosalyn McGillivay, *Western Folklore* 47 [1988]: 69–70).

20. Robert Cantwell, "Of Kings' Treasuries," *The New England Review* 14 (1991): 192.

21. Claude Lévi-Strauss, *The Savage Mind* (Chicago: University of Chicago Press, 1966), 13–14.

22. In what has been described as "the most widely cited article on folklore in the 1970's," Dan Ben-Amos reads tradition to mean antiquity and on that ground decides that "the traditional character of folklore is an analytical construct. It is a scholarly and not a cultural fact" ("Toward a Definition of Folklore in Context," in *Toward New Perspectives in Folklore,* ed. Américo Paredes and Richard Bauman [Austin: University of Texas Press, 1972], 13). Ben-Amos defines folklore as "artistic communication in small groups."

23. William F. H. Nicolaisen, "Names and Narratives," *Journal of American Folklore* 97 (1984): 268.

24. A wag has put it this way:

> D'ya wanna know the creed'a
> Jacques Derrida?
> Dere ain't no reada
> Dere ain't no wrida
> Eida.

25. For a recent instance of our recurring concern about extreme individualism in the United States, see Robert N. Bellah et al., eds. *Habits of the Heart: Individualism and Commitment in American Life* (Berkeley: University of California Press, 1985).

26. Richard Bauman, *Story, Performance, and Event: Contextual Studies of Oral Narrative* (Cambridge: Cambridge University Press, 1986), 78.

27. Walt Whitman, "Slang in America," in *Walt Whitman: Complete Poetry and Collected Prose,* ed. Justin Kaplan (New York: Library of America, 1982), 1166.

28. See Judith Lynn Hanna, *To Dance Is Human* (University of Texas Press, 1980). Among the worst embarrassments for a student in a classroom is to be asked to sing a song. The only more mortifying experience is to be asked to dance.

29. See Norman Mailer's study, *The Faith of Graffiti* (New York: Praeger, 1974); documented by Mervyn Kurlansky and Jon Naar.

30. The creative force in children, of course, is not always benign and innocent. It may very well be the expression of an underlying evil disposition. And it needn't necessarily emanate from normal children, as we have

seen in many recent instances of idiot savants. In order to make up for the imbalance he saw in providing the full range of folk creativity, Henry Glassie produced a long study of a composed song, "Take That Night Train to Selma," a racist, anti-civil rights diatribe. There is nothing wrong with documenting what Glassie calls these "sometimes quantitatively dominant, conservative fibers" in folk tradition. But their limitations are sharply revealed when compared with the tradition of classic black spirituals and contemporary civil rights songs like "We Shall Overcome." The latter has become a world-wide anthem for human freedom; "The Last Train" has long since completed its final ride. See Henry Glassie, Edward D. Ives, and John F. Szwed, *Folksongs and Their Makers* (Bowling Green, Ohio: Bowling Green University Popular Press, n.d.).

31. Lester J. Cappon, ed., *The Adams-Jefferson Papers* (Chapel Hill: University of North Carolina Press, 1959), 2: 388–89.

32. I have often witnessed the futile attempts of symphony musicians to imitate the styles of folk fiddlers. For one thing, the trained musicians are helpless without notes in front of them. At the same time, the folk styles demand disciplines very different from those taught in the academies. The circumstances validate Lévi-Strauss's argument that the processes of the folk mind in its complexities are essentially the same as those of "civilized" societies. It's also worth noting that the title *The Savage Mind* is an unfortunate translation from the French, *La Pensée sauvage.* What Lévi-Strauss means throughout is *mythic thought*—which would have been a more accurate title. It is just that human quality which remains constant in our species.

33. Cleanth Brooks, *William Faulkner: Toward Yoknapatawpha and Beyond* (New Haven: Yale University Press, 1978), 332.

## Two   Herder and Folk Ideology

1. Robert T. Clark, Jr., *Herder: His Life and Thought* (Berkeley: University of California Press, 1969), 249.

2. It is significant that unlike many of his contemporaries (including Goethe), Herder welcomed the French Revolution and its liberating energies.

3. F. M. Barnard, *Herder's Social and Political Thought* (Oxford: Clarendon Press, 1965), 70–71.

4. Clark, *Herder,* 148.

5. Quoted in F. M. Barnard, ed., *J. G. Herder on Social and Political Culture* (London: Cambridge University Press, 1969), 41. Herder anticipated the slogan of a recent anthropological congress, "One race, many cultures."

6. Clark, *Herder,* 260. The work is best known as *Stimmen der Völker in Liedern* (*Voices of the People in Song*), the title given it by Herder's editors.

7. Thomas Percy, *Reliques of Ancient English Poetry,* in Sigrid Bernhard Hustvedt, *Ballad Books and Ballad Men* (Cambridge: Harvard University Press, 1930), 23.

8. Herder in Robert Ergang, *Herder and the Foundations of German Nationalism* (New York: Columbia University Press, 1931), 200–201.

9. Barnard, *Herder's Social and Political Thought,* 70.

10. Clark, *Herder,* 66–67.

11. Ergang, *Herder and the Foundations of German Nationalism,* 162, 165.

12. Ibid., 204, 528–29.

13. Ibid., 162, 165.

14. Herder, *Outlines of a Philosophy of the History of Man,* trans. T. Churchill, 2d ed. (London: Johnson, 1803). This is still the only edition available in English. Emerson was familiar with both editions of Churchill's translation.

15. Ergang, *Herder and the Foundations of German Nationalism,* 205.

16. Clark, *Herder,* 259.

17. Isaiah Berlin, *Vico and Herder: Two Studies in the History of Ideas* (1976; London: Chatto, 1980), 193.

18. Clark, *Herder,* 128–29.

19. Someone on the writing staff of the TV show *M\*A\*S\*H* must have studied German literature and thus named the lovable transvestite on the show Max Klinger.

20. T. S. Eliot, "American Literature and Language," in *To Criticize the Critic* (New York: Farrar, 1965), 54–56. Although Eliot is usually associated with a "highbrow" tradition of criticism, he often shows the influence of Herder's attempt to balance carefully the implications of national and international values. (He takes a similar approach in his famous essay "Tradition and the Individual Talent.")

21. *Interviews with Robert Frost,* ed. Edwin Connery Latham (New York: Holt, Rinehart and Winston, 1966), 7.

22. Berlin, *Vico and Herder,* 170–71.

23. Barnard, *Herder on Social and Political Culture,* 29.

24. James Marsh, trans., *The Spirit of Hebrew Poetry,* 2 vols. (1833; reprint, Naperville, Ill.: Aleph Press, 1971), 5.

25. Cited in Clark, *Herder,* 281. In *The Spirit of Hebrew Poetry,* one of the characters in a dialogue that appears in the first part attacks the Hebrew language itself as barbaric. The character who speaks for Herder provides an eloquent defense.

26. Barnard, *Herder on Social and Political Culture,* 8–9.

27. Ibid., 22–23.

28. Berlin has noted that "If Herder's notion of the equal validity of incommensurable cultures is accepted, the concepts of an ideal state or of an ideal man become incoherent. This is a far more radical denial of the foundations of traditional morality than any Hume ever uttered" (*Vico and Herder,* 209).

29. Alex Haley, *Roots* (New York: Doubleday, 1976).

30. As Melville Herskovits pointed out in *The Myth of the Negro Past* (Boston: Beacon, 1941), African Americans were thought to be literally without a cultural heritage as a consequence of having been abducted from many different tribal groups and prohibited from practicing their inherited traditions during slavery times. The very term African American was introduced recently to counter such prejudices.

31. My first article on Herder was "Herder's Folksong Ideology," *Southern Folklore Quarterly* 6 (1962): 137–44. It was followed by "The Advantages of Barbarism: Herder and Whitman's Nationalism," *Journal of the History of Ideas* 24 (1963): 115–26.

32. In a syndicated column, Edwin M. Yoder, Jr., has suggested that "as the Cold War fades, the German question may well replace it. Historically, that question was the ultimate expression of a worldwide 19th-century cult of romantic nationalism, a nationalism of language, ethnic identity and geographical aspiration of which even the young United States caught a virulent case in the form of 'Manifest Destiny'" (Fresno *Bee,* 20 November 1989). None of these attitudes is authentically Herderian. In a study of oral narrative, Richard Bauman criticized the idea that folklore is a bastard discipline ("anthropology begot upon English"), arguing that "modern folklore has a fully honorable heritage; the seminal figure was that great precursor of romantic nationalism, Johann Gottfried von Herder" (*Story, Performance, and Event: Contextual Studies of Oral Narrative* [Cambridge: Cambridge University Press, 1986], 1). The footnote accompanying this comment deals with the nature of oral tradition; there is no reference to any work of Herder's, or any biography, or any critical study of Herder's significance. It is the only mention of Herder in the volume.

33. Albert B. Friedman, *The Ballad Revival* (Chicago: University of Chicago Press, 1961), 185. Isaiah Berlin, Robert Clark, Jr., Robert Ergang, and F. M. Barnard are among the few scholars who have consistently understood Herder accurately and actively endeavored to correct the misreadings. But the miscomprehensions continue. The following is from a discussion of Paul de Man's early anti-Semitic leanings: "There is a strong aestheticist, communitarian dimension of the appeal of Hitler's version of fascism. The recourse to nation solves with brutal simplicity a set of problems that are much too complex to be given such a single overarching solution. With their mass rallies and festivals the Nazis offered the sim-

ulacrum of a reconciliation of the opposing poles of modern political order, the individual and the collective. The Nazi aesthetic seems both to pre-serve and to overcome the isolation of the individual in modern life. This is one of the reasons why the nation becomes so important in order. We see in many of the texts of de Man from this period how important nationalism was. Two essays give voice to explicit anti-Semitism, but many are per-vaded with cultural nationalism. Such nationalism differs from National Socialism in certain ways. For the National Socialist, race, blood, is the most important factor in politics. For the aesthetic nationalist—it is a way of thinking that goes back to Herder and the romantics—it is aesthetics, culture, that determines national politics because it is the source of iden-tity, but it can be as anti-Semitic as Nazism" (Lindsay Waters, ed., *Paul de Man: Critical Writings, 1953–1978* [Minneapolis: University of Minnesota Press, 1989], xxvi). The vague "its" in the closing sentences are a source of major confusion but the overall effect is to place Herder squarely in an ugly context. Nothing could be further from the truth.

### Three   Herder and American Folk Tradition

1. Robert Clark, *Herder: His Life and Thought* (Berkeley: University of California Press, 1969), 252.

2. Alfred North Whitehead, *Science and the Modern World* (New York: Macmillan, 1925), 75–76. Sooner or later these assumptions were bound to be called into question. This is what happened when Karl Marx and Frie-drich Engels, using the data drawn by the American ethnologist Lewis Henry Morgan from the social organization of American Indians, punc-tured the notion that property rights were eternal laws of nature.

3. Isaiah Berlin, *Vico and Herder: Two Studies in the History of Ideas* (1976; London: Chatto, 1980), 181.

4. Clark, *Herder,* 323.

5. F. M. Barnard, ed., *J. G. Herder on Social and Political Culture* (London: Cambridge University Press, 1969), 5.

6. Clark, *Herder,* 335.

7. Berlin, *Vico and Herder,* p. 185.

8. Stowe, cited in Clark, *Herder,* 294. Herder himself noted, "When I read the Old Testament, I become a Jew."

9. Joel Porte, ed., *Emerson: Essays and Lectures* (New York: Library of America, 1983), 22.

10. Ibid.

11. Justin Kaplan, ed., *Walt Whitman: Complete Poetry and Collected Prose* (New York: Library of America, 1982), 672.

12. Cited in ibid., 1165–66.

13. Ibid., 1168.

14. Joseph J. Kwiat, "Robert Henri and the Emerson-Whitman Tradition," *PMLA* 81 (1956): 633.

15. W. T. Lhamon, Jr., has provided a useful introduction and bibliographical note to a new edition of Rourke's 1931 *American Humor: A Study of the National Character* (Tallahassee: Florida State University Press, 1986).

16. Constance Rourke, *The Roots of American Culture and Other Essays,* ed. Van Wyck Brooks (New York: Harcourt, 1942).

17. Ibid., 45.

18. Ibid.

19. Rourke, *American Humor,* xii.

20. John A. Lomax and Alan Lomax, eds., *Folk Song: U. S. A.* (1947; reprint, New York: New American Plume, 1975), xi.

21. I have discussed the significance of the Lomaxes' work in *The Voice of the Folk: Folklore and American Literary Theory* (Amherst: University of Massachusetts Press, 1972).

22. I have discussed the influence of the ballad hegemony in *The Voice of the Folk,* Chap. 5.

23. For a stimulating discussion of the idea of ethnicity in the United States, see Werner Sollors, *Beyond Ethnicity: Consent and Descent in American Culture* (New York: Oxford University Press, 1986), Chap. 1.

24. Lomax and Lomax, *Folk Song: U.S.A.,* x. The reference is to the famous story of "John Henry," in which a legendary black steel driver accepts a challenge to compete with a steam drill. He wins but dies in the effort.

25. Lomax wrote little about the ethnic materials that he found in the field. In *Folk Song: U.S.A.* he explained, "We have confined our selection to songs in the English tongue, because we felt the rich field of songs in other languages was not yet sufficiently explored for a fair picture to be presented." Still, among his early collections was a body of work that explored Cajun and Zydeco music, the white and black creations of French-speaking Americans in southwestern Louisiana. Long an underground treasure, these recordings have recently been issued and have become a major source for understanding the newly rediscovered Cajun and Zydeco styles—*Louisiana Cajun and Creole Music, 1934: The Lomax Recordings,* Swallow LP-8003-2.

26. I think this joke comes from the repertoire of the comic Nipsy Russell. It always gets a laugh in this country, but abroad it makes no sense. Such unlikely mixtures don't occur in most other countries, just as the food tastes remain equally segregated. In China you don't go out for soul food.

27. In his fine novel, Oscar Hijuelos points out that "Cu-bop" was the

"term used to describe the fusion of Afro-Cuban music and hot be-bop Harlem jazz: "Its great practitioner was the bandleader Machito, who with Maurio Bauza and Chano Pozo hooked up with Dizzy Gillespie and Charlie Parker in the late 1940s. The American jazz players picked up the Cuban rhythms and chord progressions. Machito's orchestra, with Chico O'Farril as arranger, became famous for dazzling solos played over extended vamps called *montunos*. During these furious breaks, when drummers like Chano Pozo and players like Charlie Parker went nuts, dancers like Frank Pérez took to the center of the ballroom floor, improvising turns, dips, splits, leaps around the basic mambo steps, in the same way that musicians improvised during their solos" (*The Mambo Kings Play Songs of Love* [New York: Farrar, 1989], 29).

28. Carvel Collins, ed., *William Faulkner: Early Prose and Poetry* (Boston: Little, Brown, 1962), 89. Faulkner concluded by noting, "It can, however, come from the strength of imaginative idiom which is understandable by all who read English. Nowhere today, saving in parts of Ireland, is the English language spoken with the same earthy strength as it is in the United States; though we are as a nation, still inarticulate."

29. Cordelia Candelaria, "Hidden Complacencies," *American Poetry Review* 11, no. 6 (January–February 1989): 1.

30. Leo Marx, quoted in Denis Donoghue, *Reading America: Essays on American Literature* (New York: Knopf, 1987), 15. Donoghue was startled by Marx's position, noting that "such a formula would force us into the predicament of regarding blacks, Chinese, Puerto Ricans, and Mexicans in the U.S.A. as marginal to an official narrative." Reevaluations are occurring in all areas of American studies research. An important volume dealing with the influence of Turner's frontier thesis on the tendency to minimize the variety of literary traditions and values in the United States is David Mogen, Mark Busby, and Paul Bryant, eds., *The Frontier Experience and the American Dream: Essays on American Literature* (College Station: Texas A & M University Press, 1989).

31. Jon Pareles, "South African Pop Breaks Out," *New York Times,* February 8, 1987, sec. 2, 1.

32. Tom Schnabel, "International Bandstand," *Los Angeles Times Magazine,* January 7, 1990, 20. Schnabel lists a number of international styles that show up on records and film tracks: "Bhangra," Indian and Pakistani dance music; "Juju," fusion of Western and Nigerian (Yoruba) music; "Lambada," fusion of *merengue* and salsa from the Bahia area of Northeast Brazil with African and Caribbean influences (which looks a lot like "dirty dancing"); "Qawwali," vocal music of Islamic Sufism; "Rai," Algerian pop music which protests restrictions of Islamic fundamentalism (centered in Paris); "Soukous," contemporary dance music from Kinshasa, Zaire; "Zouk," con-

temporary dance music from the islands of Martinique and Guadeloupe. In the summer of 1989 while traveling in the People's Republic of China, I asked a French tourist what she was listening to on her Walkman. "African music," she said. "We only listen to African music in Paris these days."

33. Nazi Germany stands supremely for the first variety. But the American and French revolutions and some of the countries of Eastern Europe represent the positive images associated with national movements.

34. Arthur M. Schlesinger, Jr., "The Opening of the American Mind: Absolutism and Relativism in the American National Experience," *New York Times Book Review,* July 23, 1989, 1.

35. Ibid., 2. In *The Disuniting of America: Reflections on a Multicultural Society* (1991; reprint, New York: Norton, 1992), Schlesinger reveals a cultural panic that has struck a number of intellectuals whose instincts have led them to support the idea of multiculturalism. He argues persistently in the short study for a "shamefully overdue recognition" of the achievements of minorities "subordinated and spurned during the high noon of Anglo dominance." But on balance he is threatened by movements of "separation" and "factionalism." It would be simple if we could have both integration and ethnic identity at once. But as Herder pointed out, universal internationalism is a stage only gradually attained. *The Disuniting of America* ends with Schlesinger quoting Crèvecoeur's famous melting-pot line: " 'What then is the American, this new man? . . . Here individuals of all nations are melted into a new race of men.' Still a good answer—still the best hope." But it's easy to see that, from many points of view (including sensitivity to gender), the old formulations no longer hold.

36. Henry Glassie, *The Spirit of Folk Art: The Girard Collection at the Museum of International Folk Art* (New York: Abrams, 1989), 92.

37. Arnold Krupat, *The Voice in the Margin: Native American Literature and the Canon* (Berkeley: University of California Press, 1989), 201.

38. Paul Lawrence Rose, *Revolutionary Antisemitism in Germany from Kant to Wagner* (Princeton: Princeton University Press, 1990), 98.

39. Ibid., 99.

40. Ibid., 108.


Four   **Poplore**

1. The question of African influence on formal (or classical) music is more complicated. Aaron Copland once commented that he thought of using the blues as a major source for symphonic composition but decided that it was too short a form. In light of lengthy improvisations (often much longer than symphonic durations) by jazz musicians, that does not seem

to be a convincing argument. Most approaches by composers using folk sources are mainly along the line of quoting folk materials rather than (as in Bartok's use of folk materials) developing new insights on the basis of the folk traditions. From earliest times to the controversy over "rap" music, white critics have persistently been appalled by the sounds as well as the ideological implications of black folk and popular music. Even experimentalists like Philip Glass and Laurie Anderson stay pretty clear of African-American sources.

2. Gerald Mullin, *Flight and Rebellion,* cited in Eugene D. Genovese, *Roll, Jordan, Roll* (1974; reprint, New York: Vintage-Random, 1976), 432. At the same time, black dialects as well as black English locutions persist to the present day. Gordon Brotherston argues that the Cherokee "diagnose the blue of the north, the direction from which the worst invaders came, as the source of trouble—what became (via Cherokee-speaking Africans) the Mississippi blues." *Book of the Fourth World: Reading the Native Americas through their Literature* (Cambridge: Cambridge University Press, 1992), 311.

3. *Journal of American Folklore* 1 (1888): 3. Other endangered species were American Indians and French Canadians. The prospectus concluded about black materials, "Such inquiries are becoming difficult, and in a few years will be impossible" (5).

4. Melville J. Herskovits, *The Myth of the Negro Past* (Boston: Beacon, 1941).

5. Dena J. Epstein, *Sinful Tunes and Spirituals: Black Folk Music to the Civil War* (Urbana: University of Illinois Press, 1977). Subsequent references will be given in the text.

6. It seems clear that the early versions of the instrument were made from gourds and had four strings, three long ones and one short string, as shown in the watercolor, "The Old Plantation" (artist unknown), dated between 1790 and 1800. The painting is in the Abby Aldrich Rockefeller Collection of American Folk Art and has been widely reproduced. Since the turn of the century, the manufacture of banjos has been a highly industrialized procedure, sometimes combined with individual craftsmanship.

7. As a source of black-to-white exchange, Epstein has noted the influence of what was known in the eighteenth century as "African or Negro Jigs." Throughout the century, whites and blacks danced these jigs which, though often described as irregular, fanatical, or lascivious, were also apparently irresistible. These jigs mark the beginnings of what has continued to be a white fascination with black dance styles. Jig is an Irish dance, but the word has also survived as a slang, derogatory term for a black person, probably through association with the slave dances.

8. "On the Field and Work of a Journal of American Folk-Lore," *Journal of American Folklore* 1 (1888):4.

9. Alan Jabbour, ed., *American Fiddle Tunes From the Archive of Folk Song*, Library of Congress, Washington, D.C., 1971, AFS L62, 1.

10. Ibid., 12.

11. Robert C. Toll, *Blacking Up: The Minstrel Show in Nineteenth-Century America* (New York: Oxford University Press, 1974), 42. Subsequent references will be given in the text.

12. Hans Nathan, *Dan Emmett and the Rise of Early Negro Minstrelsy* (Norman: Oklahoma University Press, 1962), 207. Subsequent references will be given in the text. The syncopation, Nathan has explained, "is of historical significance because it provided elements from which, later on, rags, blues, and finally jazz developed their idiom. The motion . . . is animated by many irregular stresses: hectic offbeat accentuations projected against the relentless, metrical background of the accompanying taps [of the performer's foot], which changes ¾ into ⅛. A large number of accentuations result from brief, sudden rests on one of the four beats in the measure" (195). Nathan has maintained that American banjo music begins with "back country" British tradition, "but from it banjo music proceeded to an idiom infinitely more complex in rhythm than could have originated within a predominantly white cultural milieu and its nineteenth-century concepts" (207). The same can be said about fiddling styles.

13. "Though firmly rooted in Euro-American musical and dance tradition these white minstrels affected both white and black America: first and foremost they revolutionized the white structure of feeling by creating a taste for black culture in their audience and secondly they opened the market for black minstrels. . . . Out of their combined efforts emerged certain forms of popular culture: burlesque, stand-up comedy, ragtime and cakewalk blues, surrealist nonsense, coon songs, and black minstrel tunes. It was this culture which provided the subsoil and market of the emerging jazz music" (Berndt Ostendorf, *Black Literature in White America* [Brighton, Sussex: Harvester Press, 1982], 87).

14. Eric Lott, " 'The Seeming Counterfeit': Racial Politics and Early Blackface Minstrelsy," *American Quarterly* 43 (1991): 226–27.

15. See David Mogen, Mark Busby, and Paul Bryant, eds., *The Frontier Experience and the American Dream: Essays on American Literature* (College Station: Texas A & M University Press, 1989). The editors are concerned with the conventional Anglo, masculine emphasis in Turner's approach and try to establish a dialogue through responses by women and minority groups.

16. Frederick Jackson Turner, *The Frontier in American History* (1920; reprint, New York: Holt, 1962), 4.

17. Consider, as one of many examples, the Boy Scouts of America, whose military garb masks its major reliance on native American (*scout*) approaches and materials.

18. See my discussion of the "Arkansas Traveler" strategy of humor in *The Voice of the Folk,* Chap. 4. For the classic formulation of "paleface and redskin," see Philip Rahv, *Essays on Literature and Politics: 1932–1972,* ed. Arabel J. Porter and Andrew J. Dvosin (Boston: Houghton Mifflin, 1978), 3–7.

19. I have been disputing Sweeney's claim for many years. But since the widespread popularity of a watercolor, "The Old Plantation" (see note 6), there is little doubt that his claim is unfounded. The work shows a group of slaves, among them one playing a gourd banjo with four strings; one of these strings is a drone string like the fifth string of the later banjo. It's obvious that the principle of a high drone string is a folk and ultimately African creation that clearly predates Sweeney's argument that he invented the fifth string in the 1820s. It has been suggested that Sweeney may have added the fourth, low string on the banjo.

20. William J. Mahar has shown convincingly that "rather than being solely a vehicle for white prejudice," blackface characters were used to "create reverse images—like the image of a photographer's negative—of the most cherished American values or of the true differences between American life and its social or cultural ideals." While surely racist, minstrelsy also injected "a vital, discordant, and satirical language into popular comedy. The similarities between the black and white 'Frontiersmen's' rhetoric as well as the shared use of 'boasts' or 'toasts' in the respective cultures suggest a common human ground underlying all antebellum humor" ("Black England in Early Blackface Minstrelsy: A New Interpretation of the Sources of Minstrel Show Dialect," *American Quarterly* 37 (1985): 284–85. In *Way Up North in Dixie: A Black Family's Claim to the Confederate Anthem* (Washington, D.C., Smithsonian Institution Press, 1993). Howard L. Sacks and Judith Rose Sacks claim that "Dixie" was inspired and perhaps even written, in part or in full, by a black musical family named the Snowdens, who lived in the same neck of the Ohio woods where Dan Emmett was born and, late in life, returned to die.

21. Gilbert Chase, *America's Music: From the Pilgrims to the Present* (New York: McGraw Hill, 1955), 278. Subsequent references will be given in the text.

22. For the literary materials that preceded Mark Twain's accomplishments, see Walter Blair, *Native American Humor* (1937; reprint, San Francisco: Chandler, 1960). Edmund Wilson's *Patriotic Gore: Studies in the Literature of the American Civil War* (1962; reprint, New York: Oxford-Galaxy, 1966) also shows clearly the emergence of a new canon from the same poplore mixture.

23. Although the tune may be folk in origin, the words were composed by an Englishman, John Newton, a former slave captain who became an evangelist. The version of the song transcribed by Charles and Ruth Seeger in John Lomax and Alan Lomax, *Folk Song: U.S.A.* (1947; reprint, New York: New American-Plume, 1975), shows the ornamentation of black folk style.

24. The legendary Appalachian singer Jean Ritchie has described to me the ornamentation of songs in her singing family's tradition as "relishing the tune." See her family history, *The Singing Family of the Cumberlands* (1955; reprint, New York: Oak, 1963).

25. In Lomax and Lomax, *Folk Song: U.S.A.,* 418.

26. Ibid., 18.

27. Chase states "Charles Wesley's hymn deserved this treatment, for he is said to have written it as a parody on a popular song celebrating the return to England of Admiral Vernon (after whom Washington's Mount Vernon was named) following the capture of Portobello in 1739. As for the tune, it belongs to a type that has enjoyed wide circulation in America's music, from the folk hymns of the fasola singers to the minstrel songs of Stephen Foster" (214).

28. In William C. Dowling, *Jameson, Althusser, Marx: An Introduction to the Political Unconscious* (Ithaca, N.Y.: Cornell University Press, 1984), 132.

29. Dorson made it very clear that conservatism for him was a political as well as a philosophical position, insisting "it is no business of the folklorist to engage in social reform . . . he will become the poorer scholar and folklorist if he turns activist." Quoted by Timothy H. Evans, "Folklore vs. Utopia: English Medievalists and the Ideology of Revivalism," *Western Folklore* 47 (1988): 263.

30. One of Mark Twain's central accomplishments was his ability to use both black and white dialects accurately and lucidly. Unlike the earlier southwestern writers who employed orthographic humor to poke fun at their rustic characters, Twain found just the right balance, providing the sense of the language without ridiculing the culture it came from. Hemingway and Faulkner, among many others, continued this tradition of handling vernacular speech with respect.

31. The references range from Genesis to the Book of Revelation. See Epstein's discussion of *Slave Songs of the United States* (1867), the first collection of black spirituals. "Go Down, Moses" was one of the many songs included in the volume.

32. Charles Joyner, review of C. Vann Woodward, *The Encyclopedia of Southern Culture,* in *New York Review of Books,* February 15, 1990, 52.

33. Lawrence W. Levine, *Black Culture and Black Consciousness: Afro-American Folk Thought from Slavery to Freedom* (New York: Oxford University Press, 1977), 135.

34. Henry Louis Gates, Jr., *The Signifying Monkey: A Theory of African-American Literary Criticism* (New York: Oxford University Press, 1988), 50.

35. Levine, *Black Culture,* 19.

36. My colleague Professor Phyllis A. Irwin has pointed out to me that basic phrases from "We Shall Overcome" are in a Catholic hymn, "O Sanctissima," as well as in Protestant church hymns. There is also a German Christmas carol that uses the tune. Reverend Gary Davis recorded a version that uses exactly the same tune with the words, "I'll be all right." (*Reverend Gary Davis: A Little More Faith,* Prestige/Bluesville, n.d.)

37. Jocelyn Y. Stewart, "Tutu Calls U.S. Rights Struggle Inspiring," Los Angeles *Times,* May 14, 1990, B 1.

### Five   Folklore, Fakelore, and Poplore

1. I came to Michigan State University in East Lansing just after Dorson had left for Indiana. MSU was furious at his having left and accused him of stealing a tape recorder and the MSU "folk archives." I don't know about the former, but the latter turned out to be Dorson's file cabinet of his own collections. A colleague I met there who was a good talker but not a great publisher of articles quoted Dorson's advice to him: "Don't talk about it; can it and publish it." Dorson's huge publication list is testimony to his having taken his own advice seriously.

2. Richard M. Dorson, "Folklore, Academe, and the Marketplace," in *Folklore and Fakelore: Essays toward a Discipline of Folk Studies* (Cambridge: Harvard University Press, 1976), 5. Subsequent references will be given in the text. Without naming the author, Dorson referred to a use of the term in an article that he said appeared in 1970 in the *Saturday Review* entitled, "Folklore, Fakelore, and Poplore." Actually it was written by Marshall Fishwick (26 August 1967, 20ff.). Fishwick does indeed follow Dorson's meaning of fakelore. "From the kaleidoscopic variety of subforms," he maintained, "comes the new sound of poplore: a celebration of the new, plugged in, revved-up psychedelic global village in which we must somehow find our way" (43).

3. Alan Dundes, *Folklore Matters* (Knoxville: University of Tennessee Press, 1989), 40, 42. Subsequent references will be given in the text.

4. William A. Wilson, *Folklore and Nationalism in Modern Finland* (Bloomington: Indiana University Press, 1976), 40. Quoted in Dundes, *Folklore Matters,* 46.

5. Although we never met, it was very clear that my work was on Dorson's mind, especially since I began criticizing his conception of fakelore quite early. At a meeting of the Popular Culture Association in 1973 devoted to a discussion of my book, *The Voice of the Folk: Folklore and*

*American Literary Theory,* my criticism of fakelore drew almost hysterical denunciation from some of Dorson's students who were at the session. (The meeting took place in Indianapolis, very close to Dorson's home ground.) My mild criticism of his contribution to a book on urban folklore apparently threw more fuel on the fire.

6. Like many historians at the time, Dorson was very upset with what came to be known as the "myth and symbol" school of criticism, especially when Henry Nash Smith won a major history award for his book, *Virgin Land: The American West as Symbol and Myth* (1950). Although Smith and Leo Marx were my teachers at the University of Minnesota, neither had much background in folklore and none in folk song, which was my main interest and the focus of my doctoral thesis. I owe them both a great debt, nevertheless, and acknowledged it in *The Voice of the Folk.*

7. Dorson was well aware of my extensive field experience, but like many conventional academic folklorists, he tends to negate work in the area of folk song and folk music as somehow not quite a legitimate activity. I think it's partly from his own weakness in the area and also from the concern that folk song has been so commercialized as to raise constantly the specter of fakelore.

8. Denisoff's book, *Great Day Coming: Folk Music and the American Left* (Urbana: University of Illinois Press, 1971), was an ill-informed attack on Guthrie, Seeger, Alan Lomax, Paul Robeson, Bob Dylan, and many other politically minded performers. It sounded very much like a compendium from *Red Channels* and other right-wing reports. A second edition is toned down considerably.

9. It was Ma Joad in *The Grapes of Wrath* who is at first puzzled and then hurt by the epithet "Okie" when she encounters it in California. Although some descendants of thirties' migrant workers ignore the negative connotations of the term, others are still deeply offended by it. Joe Klein, in *Woody Guthrie: A Life* (New York: Knopf, 1980), 164, states that Woody "touched millions . . . the migrant workers and Okies to, and about whom, he sang."

10. Although the word bluegrass is widely used to mean any country or folk-sounding music, it is actually a technical term which refers to a style invented around 1945 by mandolinist Bill Monroe. When Earl Scruggs brought his lightning-fast five-string banjo picking style to Monroe's group, the Bluegrass Boys (named after their Kentucky origins), the style was complete. Both Monroe and Scruggs used traditional materials to develop their highly innovative approaches to instrumental and vocal techniques. The history and meaning of bluegrass are documented fully by Robert Cantwell in *Bluegrass Breakdown: The Making of the Old Southern Sound* (Urbana: University of Illinois Press, 1984). Cantwell's metaphysical mus-

ings are equally interesting. He has concluded that "instrumentally and vocally bluegrass music is a thoroughgoing 'process of rhythm,' an Afro-American ensemble form in the body of traditional Appalachian music" (273).

11. See the discussion of Kazee's career in the Appendix.

12. Kazee had written a folk opera based on hymn tunes, some of which I included in my documentary Folkways album, *Buell Kazee Sings and Plays,* where he also performed some pop tunes.

13. Ruth Crawford Seeger's avant-garde compositions have only recently been receiving attention. See Judith Tick, "Ruth Crawford's 'Spiritual Concept': The Sound-Ideals of an Early Modernist," *Journal of the American Musicological Society* 44 (1991): 221–61. Tick deals with the composer's interests in Theosophy and Eastern and American transcendentalism, including the ideas of Walt Whitman.

14. Pete Seeger, *The Incompleat Folksinger,* ed. Jo Metcalf Schwartz (New York: Simon, 1972), 13. Subsequent references will be given in the text.

15. *How To Play the 5-String Banjo* was published in 1961 and distributed by Oak Publications. A record and instruction book were published by Folkways Records (8303).

16. In the 1960s when almost no five-string banjos were being manufactured by the companies who were famous for making them in the past, Vega began to produce the Pete Seeger model, a long-necked banjo that had become Seeger's trademark. The Scruggs bluegrass model wasn't introduced until 1987.

17. Seeger characteristically credits Earl Scruggs with inspiring thousands of young people to play the five-string banjo in the "syncopated version of the old 'clawhammer' finger-picking style" associated with bluegrass music and still known as "Scruggs style banjo." But it was Seeger's more traditional approach that started the banjo revival and still intrigues many amateur players.

18. The five-string banjo is a major case in point, having experienced several stages of development by younger artists who have emphasized chromatic approaches and virtuoso picking techniques with dazzling proficiency. At the same time there are many players in traditional style whose work cannot be distinguished from that of the older performers.

19. Karen Linn, *That Half-Barbaric Twang: The Banjo in American Popular Culture* (Urbana: University of Illinois Press, 1991), 153. Only one contemporary black musician plays the five-string banjo in traditional style. Taj Mahal has argued for many years that blacks should reclaim the instrument that was their original contribution to our culture. For most African Americans, the banjo is still too closely associated with the slavery apologetics of the minstrel tradition and with black stereotypes.

20. See Linn's descriptions of attempts to "elevate" the banjo by associating it with genteel traditions and by marketing it as an appropriate instrument for young ladies.

21. Seeger's banjo repertoire featured black spirituals as well as blues. It revealed that the banjo is indeed the source for a main black blues style, represented by many traditional bottle-neck blues musicians whose picking styles and use of open tunings show clearly their familiarity with banjo technique. I have rarely spoken with traditional blues artists who did not mention playing the banjo early in their lives, though none would do so in public.

22. Both Klein and Seeger provide good discussions of the organization and function of the Almanac Singers, which included Seeger, Guthrie, Lee Hays, Millard Lampell, Butch Hawes, and Bess Lomax.

23. Of course, the influence of Guthrie and Seeger on labor is not entirely negligible. Union songs such as Guthrie's "Union Maid" and others propagated by left-wing artists are still often sung by union members. And to this day, Pete Seeger can be counted on to show up at any picket line in the country where his services are requested. See Robbie Lieberman's, *My Song Is My Weapon* (Urbana: University of Illinois Press, 1989).

24. A major collection of such materials is in John Greenway, *American Folksongs of Protest* (Philadelphia: University of Pennsylvania Press, 1953). The date of publication reveals Greenway's courage in associating himself with a tradition then under furious attack by politicians as well as academics. He quoted a typical academic response to protest materials: "The truest values of folklore, which are entertainment for the participants, or as the materials for cultural studies by the scholar, are completely lost or perverted" (4). I once taught "Pastures of Plenty," Guthrie's brilliant song about the migrant workers in the 1930s, to a group of United Farm Workers in Fresno, and they immediately added two verses in Spanish. The version can be heard on The Bluestein Family recording, *Sowin' On the Mountain* (Philo/Fretless).

25. Seeger heard the song first from Zilphia Horton; it was a strike version of an older black church tune, often sung, "I'll Overcome." Seeger changed it to "We Shall Overcome." Later Guy Carawan began singing the song in the South and reviving it for civil rights occasions. Ultimately the song was rendered in YMCA style, with the audience linking arms as they sang.

26. Popular versions (including an airlines commercial that aired after Guthrie's death) never include the radical stanzas:

> Was a big high wall there that tried to stop me
> A sign was painted said, Private Property.

> But on the back side, it didn't say nothing—
> This land was made for you and me.

> One bright sunny morning in the shadow of the steeple
> By the relief office I saw my people—
> As they stood there hungry,
> I stood there wondering if
> This land was made for you and me.

The last line of each verse was originally, "God blessed America for me." See Klein, *Woody Guthrie,* 141.

27. Working closely with Folkways Records founder Moe Asch, Seeger has left an impressive collection of recordings to illustrate the traditions that have interested him. The result has been an influence that transcends the field of folklore and has made a significant impact on popular audiences throughout the world. Unlike the watered-down versions of the Weavers' commercial recordings, the Folkways recordings show Seeger at his most effective and uninhibited; they range from topical, political compilations to such playful innovations as the "Goofing Off Suite." All these are still available in the Folkways catalogue, now distributed by the Smithsonian Institution.

28. Sally Price, *Primitive Art in Civilized Places* (Chicago: University of Chicago Press, 1989), 37. Subsequent references will be given in the text. It's important to recall that one of the effects of Herder's relativism is to prevent such facile universalist ideologies, which actually privilege the values of "civilized" societies.

29. Jean Ritchie, *Singing Family of the Cumberlands* (1955; reprint, New York: Oak, 1963), 16. Subsequent references will be given in the text. The reprint retains the original illustrations by Maurice Sendak.

30. It is likely that black railroad workers also brought the five-string banjo into the mountains. It would ultimately become the characteristic instrument of the Southern Appalachians, as I have pointed out in *The Voice of the Folk.*

31. The term hillbilly, once a derogatory term, is now widely used by folklorists to refer to the commercial, southern white stringbands who were popular during the 1920s. Their music became one of the main sources of country western and bluegrass developments. Successful country musicians often joke: "They used to call me hillbilly, but since I sold a million records, I'm known as Mountain William." A pioneering issue of the *Journal of American Folklore,* edited by D. K. Wilgus and John Greenway, 78 (1965), attempted to convince folklorists that hillbilly music was worth investigating.

32. There were actually many indications of change in the family experi-

ence. Ritchie's father had bought a second-hand printing press and among his projects was "a little booklet of old songs which he named, *Lover's Melodies, A Choice Collection of Old Sentimental Songs Our Grandmothers Sang, and Other Popular Airs*. It sold for ten cents and contained twenty songs, among them, 'Casey Jones,' 'Blue Bells of Scotland,' 'Kitty Wells,' and old Scottish-English ballads like 'Jackaro,' 'The Brown Girl,' 'Sweet Willie,' 'Lonesome Turtledove,' 'The Printer's Bride,' and 'A Foreign Lander' " (76).

33. Occasionally one gets a glimmer of the real sources of our culture, as in the following news service note: "Roger Miller says African-American blues guitarists and fiddlers were an important influence on white country musicians in the 1920s. 'I think we need to give black people more credit for their role in country music,' said Miller, who gained fame with his hit 'King of the Road' in the 1960s" (Fresno *Bee,* 11 June 1990).

34. Ritchie noted that both the smaller and larger sizes were made by local crafts people. Her choice determined the models that were made thereafter.

35. Both the standard styles of plucking with a feather (later she began using picks cut from margarine tub lids, explaining that turkey feathers were not what they used to be) and finger-picking melodies became widely popular. But it is interesting to note her reaction to those who began to use chords with the left hand instead of relying on the open tunings traditionally employed. "If they want to play guitar style," she has commented to me on many occasions, "they're better off using a guitar instead of a dulcimer." It's a way of arguing that one can't simply do anything that one pleases with the traditional styles. Some innovations just don't work.

36. Groups such as the Kingston Trio and others who attempted to cash in on the popularity of the Weavers show clearly that just holding a banjo or guitar in one's hands does not guarantee any fidelity to the folk styles suggested by the titles of the songs performed. At the same time, I prefer poplore to the term indigenous literature that Arnold Krupat, in *The Voice in the Margin: Native American Literature and the Canon* (Berkeley: University of California Press, 1989) uses for very much the same idea applied to contemporary Native American traditions: "*Indigenous literature* I propose as the term for that form of literature which results from the *interaction* of local, internal, traditional, tribal, or 'Indian' literary modes with the dominant literary modes of the various nation-states in which it may appear" (214).

37. Along with the dozens of traditional songs Ritchie has kept alive in concerts and her many recordings, some of her widely sung compositions include, "The L&N Don't Stop Here Any More," "Black Waters," "High Hills and Mountains," and "The Cool of the Day." Bob Dylan used one of her tunes for his "Masters of War"; it took the threat of a lawsuit to convince

him to acknowledge it. A trio of country singers sang her song "My Dear Companion" on a million-selling album.

38. Linn, *That Half-Barbaric Twang,* 131–32.

## Conclusion

1. Ralph Waldo Emerson, "Historic Notes of Life and Letters in New England," in *The Portable Emerson,* ed. Carl Bode and Malcolm Cowley (New York: Penguin, 1981).

2. In response to a number of attacks on deconstruction from American academics, Jacques Derrida has commented, "Furthermore, contrary to what is so often thought, deconstruction is not exported from Europe to the United States. Deconstruction has several original configurations in this country, which in turn—and there are many signs of this—produce singular effects in Europe and elsewhere in the world. . . . Were I not so frequently associated with this adventure of deconstruction, I would risk, with a smile, the following hypothesis: America *is* deconstruction (l'Amérique mais *c'est* la deconstruction)." Derrida means that "deconstruction and America are two open sets which intersect partially" (*Mémoires: for Paul de Man,* trans. Cecile Lindsay, Jonathan Culler, and Eduardo Cadava [New York: Columbia University Press, 1986], 14, 18).

3. The history of American literature, for example, reveals a steady movement away from European influences in the direction of a canon that highlights the major ethnic groups from Native Americans to the most recent immigrants from Asia and elsewhere in an almost unlimited combination of cultural elements. The quest for "the great American novel" is an illusion. There will be more than one.

4. Nathan Gardels, "Two Concepts of Nationalism: An Interview with Isaiah Berlin," *New York Review of Books,* November 21, 1991, 19–23.

5. Ibid., 19.

6. Louis Menand, "Being an American: How the United States is Becoming Less, Not More Diverse," *Times Literary Supplement,* October 30, 1992, 4.

7. That does not mean, of course, that we have no interest in classical literature and philosophy or that we need to reject them because they were based on slave systems. But as Herder effectively explains, they are not as close to us and do not speak as powerfully as the unique tradition forged in our brief but intense history.

## Appendix One  **Moses Asch and the Legacy of Folkways Records**

1. Information on the early history of the phonograph is from Roland Gelatt, *The Fabulous Phonograph: 1877–1977,* 3d ed. (New York: Macmillan, 1977).

2. For a history of early recordings, including ethnic materials, see Richard Spottswood, *Ethnic Music on Records: A Discography of Ethnic Recordings Produced in the United States, 1893 to 1942,* 7 vols. (Urbana-Champaign: University of Illinois Press, 1990). Spottswood has also edited a special fifteen-record series, *Folk Music in America,* which includes ethnic recordings (field recordings as well as commercial products) that illustrate "the extraordinary panoply of grassroots ethnic musical traditions extant in America during the first half of the twentieth century" (xiii). "By 1906," Spottswood has noted, a "Columbia disc and cylinder catalogue could advertise records in German, Hebrew, Yiddish, French, Spanish, Czech (Bohemian), Danish, Russian, Swedish, Polish, and Hungarian" (xv).

3. Robert M. W. Dixon and John Goodrich, *Recording the Blues* (New York: Stein, 1970), 99–100. For a discussion of John and Alan Lomax's folk ideology, see Gene Bluestein, *The Voice of the Folk: Folklore and American Literary Theory* (Amherst: University of Massachusetts Press, 1972), Chap. 5. Alan Lomax has published a highly informative memoir of his fieldwork in the 1930s: *The Land Where the Blues Began* (New York: Pantheon Books, 1993).

4. See my discussion in *Anglish/Yinglish: Yiddish in American Life and Literature* (Athens: University of Georgia Press, 1989), 127–32. A comment in *The New Yorker* explains, "It'll never be as big as Bon Jovi, but klezmer music—traditional Eastern European Yiddish music—is enjoying a mini-vogue. . . . Also, if you really want to compete in the modern klezmer arena, it might help to be conversant in jazz, minimalism, and an array of international styles, because today's klezmer player is not a rube from the shtetl but an eclectic, versatile musician who is as likely to play at a downtown space as at a Jewish wedding" (July 23, 1990, 5).

5. Charles Seeger, "The Folkness of the Nonfolk and the Nonfolkness of the Folk," in *Studies in Musicology: 1935–1975* (Berkeley: University of California Press, 1977), 339. Seeger sought for a name for this combination of "folkness and nonfolkness." Since it has been in process since the beginning of our history, I suggest that poplore ought to do. His essay was first published in 1966.

6. I interviewed Moe Asch on 7 April 1978. He was a large, portly man who presented a gruff exterior. But he was anxious to talk about his life and vocation if he sensed you had some notion of what he was trying to do. When I quizzed him about his early radio experiences, he became animated and exclaimed that I was the first to catch that connection with his Folkways operation. The long interview has been edited and carefully transcribed to give a sense of Asch's characteristic tone. Moe Asch died 19 October 1986.

7. *Cowboy Songs* was first published in 1910 with a preface by Wendell Barrett and a congratulatory message from Teddy Roosevelt.

8. The call letters are after Eugene V. Debs, the socialist reformer and activist, for whom I was named.

9. *Leadbelly's Last Sessions.* See the Folkways catalogue for the several versions of these materials.

10. One of the several remarkable cantatas based on folk styles composed by Earl Robinson. The text is by Millard Lampell, who was one of the Almanac Singers along with Seeger and Woody Guthrie.

11. The Smithsonian, in conjunction with Rounder Records, is in the process of reorganizing the Folkways collection, releasing many issues on cassette. The following are the labels issued by Moe Asch:

Asch Records 1939–41, 1960–70
Asch-Stinson, 1941–46
Asch-Atlantic (with Bob Thiele), 1943–45
Disc (with Norman Granz), 1946–51
Folkways Records, 1948–86
Folkways Ethnic Library, 1948–86
Pioneer Records, 1945–48
RBF Records, 1952
Union Records, 1946

### Appendix Two   **Buell Kazee**

1. *Buell Kazee Sings and Plays* (FS 3810, 1958). Moe Asch never let an album go out of print no matter how few were sold. This album is still available through the Smithsonian Institution.

2. Notes to *Buell Kazee,* June Appal (JA 009, 1978). The record consists of a series of miscellaneous tapes and contains a full discography by Norm Cohen, based on one compiled earlier by the Australian collector John Edwards. Jones and June Appal have refused to retract these damaging claims despite extensive evidence that they are false, even after I provided them with copies of the contract, letters from Kazee encouraging the project, and proof that I received nothing for the tapes.

3. Gene Bluestein, *Songs of the North Star State* (FA 2132, 1955).

4. Kazee refers to himself in the third person throughout the interview.

5. Kazee plays "Dance Around My Pretty Little Miss" on his Folkways album.

6. This is often called a cross-tuning. It is the mixolydian forerunner of the G scale. Although it sounds "dissonant" when strummed, it works quickly into the melodies being played.

# Index